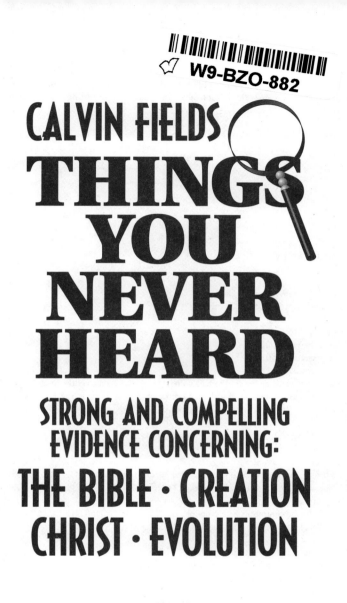

CALVIN FIELDS

THINGS YOU NEVER HEARD

STRONG AND COMPELLING EVIDENCE CONCERNING:

THE BIBLE · CREATION CHRIST · EVOLUTION

ACW Press
Phoenix, Arizona 85013

Unless otherwise noted Scripture taken from the HOLY BIBLE, NEW INTERNA-
TIONAL VERSION Copyright 1973, 1978, 1984 International Bible Society. Used by
Permission of Zondervan Bible Publishers (In some cases, the author has added **highlights**
for emphasis)

Verses marked KJV are taken from the King James Version of the Bible.

Things You Never Heard
Copyright ©2001 Calvin F. Fields
All rights reserved

Cover Design by Walljasper Design
Interior design by Pine Hill Graphics

Packaged by ACW Press
5501 N. 7th Ave., #502
Phoenix, Arizona 85013
www.acwpress.com
The views expressed or implied in this work do not necessarily reflect those of ACW Press.
Ultimate design, content, and editorial accuracy of this work is the responsibility of the
author(s).

Library of Congress Cataloging-in-Publication Data

Fields, Calvin F.
    Things you never heard: about the Bible!, creation!,
Christ!, evolution! / Calvin F. Fields. -- 1st ed.
    p. cm.
    Includes bibliographical references.
    ISBN: 1-892525-48-8

    1. Bible--Evidence, authority, etc. 2. Bible and
science. 3. Creation--Biblical teaching. 4. Human
evolution. I. Title.

BS480.F54 2001   220.1
                                 QBI01-200326

Printed in the United States of America.

DEDICATION AND
ACKNOWLEDGMENTS

CHRISTIANS ARE THE "LIGHT OF THE WORLD"! YET MOST OF THE world, almost two thousand years after Christ died, is still in darkness. Not because of Christ! Not because of His message! But because Christians have failed to convince the world that Jesus is the Son of God. Sadly, millions of young men and women within the Christian community itself have been swept away by the doctrines of men, both religious and scientific.

This book is dedicated to the task of facing some of the most basic issues believers in Christ, especially teenagers and young adults, must deal with on a daily basis. If successful, it will be a step toward Christian unity and a preservation of young minds against agnostics and atheists who abuse science to further personal agendas and biases. The book also addresses the excesses of religious doctrines, based on human opinions, that have, unknowingly, contributed to their ungodly causes. It is my fervent prayer that someday there will be an end to these divisive and weakening doctrines of men—replaced by the undivided and overwhelmingly powerful Church of the Lord Jesus Christ, **"perfectly united in mind and thought"** (1 Corinthians 1:10).

The book is also dedicated to my wonderful wife. She has patiently and helpfully endured the time and effort devoted to research and a zillion rewrites. And to the dozens of people who took the time and made the effort to give an honest critique of several drafts of the manuscript, "Thank you" seems so inadequate. May God bless these wonderful people!

Neither would the book have been written but for the love, patience and wisdom of a mother who instilled in me a "caring" for other people. Who, when she died at the age of ninety-five, was surrounded by people from all walks of life with a story about how she had helped them. As one of my cousins put it, "We would have starved if it had not been for Aunt Sylvia." Though we had little money, I never remember sitting down to eat with just our family. There were always cousins and friends, both adults and especially children.

I must also give thanks to my paternal grandfather, my buddy, who, though a poor man, gave me the immeasurable riches of unconditional love and companionship. As did the man who baptized me into Christ and taught me the value of Biblical knowledge and the joy of Christian ministry—thank you Brother Kepple! Finally, but not least, my undying appreciation to John and Ruby Glassley who gave me their daughter, my wonderful companion in every aspect of my life.

TABLE OF CONTENTS

HELP IN UNDERSTANDING
THIS BOOK

CHRISTIAN BIBLE CONSISTS OF TWO MAIN SECTIONS CALLED
ld Testament and The New Testament. The Old Testament is mostly
he history of the Jewish people. The New Testament is about Christ and
Church of Christ. The Bible is actually a library of sixty-six books and
und together for ease of study and reference. Over forty different people
over a period of about sixteen hundred years.

criptures, unless otherwise noted, are quoted from the New
nal Version of the Bible. This version was chosen because it is easier to
ially by younger readers, than most other equally acceptable transla-
rther aid the reader, verse numbers within each quotation are omit-
here feasible, quotations have been shortened by using…to indicate
tervening verses or words or [ ] to indicate an addition of words or
id in understanding (e.g. "He came as a witness…that through him
t believe…[and become] a witness to the…light" (John 1:7-9). The
appropriate, has added emphasis **highlights.**

eferences identify the book, chapter and verse where it appears in
example, Genesis 2:3-5 refers to the book of Genesis, second chapter, verses three through five. The location of each book of the Bible may be
found from a listing appearing on one of the first few pages of your personal
Bible. However, these references are generally quoted and even repeated, where
appropriate, so the readers do not have to flip back and forth in this book or
unnecessarily spend time trying to find them in their own Bible.

Prophecy is a verbal or written statement about the future. Many people, even
today, believe this power is vested in fortune-tellers and astrologers. It was a

common belief among ancient people. For this reason, God provided a method for determining who actually had this power and who did not, and a further test to determine if he or she should be followed:

> *If what a prophet proclaims in the name of the LORD does not take place or come true that is a message the LORD has not spoken. That prophet has spoken presumptuously. Do not be afraid of him* (Deuteronomy 18:22).

> *If a prophet, or one who foretells by dreams, appears among you and announces to you a miraculous sign or wonder, and if the sign or wonder of which he has spoken takes place, and he says, "Let us follow other gods (gods you have not known) and let us worship them," you must not listen to the words of that prophet or dreamer. The LORD your God is testing you to find out whether you love him with all your heart and with all your soul* (Deuteronomy 13:1-3).

Metaphor is a word, phrase or story about one thing to illustrate something else, most often some spiritual truth. For example, Jesus used "seed" to represent the "word" of God in one parable and the "children of God" in another (Matthew, chapter 13).

Culture refers to the things that different groups of people do, say or believe. Within this book it refers to the civilizations mentioned in the Bible.

Linguistic idiom refers to the language culture peculiar to the men who wrote the Bible. For example, virtually all Bible writers, in a manner similar to modern writers, used **hyperbolic expressions**, exaggerations, such as "… all those who were leaders in the world"…"the man who made the world a desert"…"the plan determined for the whole world" (Isaiah 14:9-26). These expressions do not literally mean the entire world, but rather that part of the world under the influence of the king of Babylon.

Microevolution is a limited form of change that retains the basic attributes of a particular species. This is the form accepted by religionists and scientists alike. Some prefer to identify this as "succession" or "variation" rather than evolution.

Macroevolution has no limits and is rejected by most people in the religious community. It is the form of evolution believed by many scientists as an explanation for all life-forms. This does not mean all evolutionists reject the possibility of a supernatural force called God, but they do reject the Biblical account of creation. Adherents are most often referred to as "evolutionists" or "evolutionary naturalists."

Paleontologists are scientists who study prehistoric fossils of plants and animals, including humans.

Archaeologists are scientists who study the life and cultures of ancient people.

Biologists are scientists who study "life"—such as animal and plant morphology, physiology, origin and development.

Theologians are those devoted to a study of religious doctrines.

Sin is a violation of God's laws. Adam and Eve became the first sinners when they disobeyed God and ate the forbidden fruit. For this act, they were denied access to the "tree of life" along with all their descendants. Sin also results in spiritual separation from God.

Savior is a name sometimes used when referring to Jesus Christ. He saves us from our sins and restores our spiritual relationship with God. But the most important meaning of Savior is the assurance of going to Heaven when we die— saved from an eternity of torment.

Messiah is also a name sometimes used when referring to Christ. It means the "anointed" one.

Gentiles or Greeks are terms often employed by Bible writers to identify non-Jewish people.

Moses is the name of the man God chose to write most of the Pentateuch, the first five books of the Old Testament. The first book, Genesis, will be referred to many times.

Paradigm, as used in this book, refers to the mental boxes we build that prevent us from seeing other possibilities. For example, Jesus said of the Jewish religious leaders, "Though seeing, they do not see; though hearing, they do not hear or understand" (Matthew 13:13).

Source references, whenever feasible, immediately follow quotations. Otherwise they appear as footnotes on the same page. This allows for ease of reference while reading without interrupting the train of thought.

ABOUT THE AUTHOR

CALVIN (FOR CALVIN COOLIDGE) FRANKLIN (FOR FRANKLIN Roosevelt) Fields was born in 1932 and "reared" in the mountains of West Virginia. At seven, he told his mother he would not go to school. She "reared" him all the way there. He loved learning and six years later entered high school. But, in his senior year, he dropped out. Calvin and a couple of friends had "run off" some moonshiners whiskey—without their permission! He joined the Air Force!

While in the Air Force, Calvin became an aircraft mechanic, an instructor and, during the Korean "Police Action" (seemed like a "war" to him), flew sixty-eight combat missions as a flight engineer. Among other decorations, he received the Distinguished Flying Cross for rescuing a downed fighter pilot from behind enemy lines.

After his discharge in 1953, Calvin worked as an aircraft mechanic and inspector for Boeing Aircraft Company to pay his way through college. He graduated with two degrees, Accounting and Business Administration. He then worked for and later became a partner in the C.P.A. firm of McDonald, Napshin & Shedd.

In 1965, he went to work for the Federal Aviation Administration. Among other jobs, he was the manager of accounting, budget and management systems divisions. His main job was to analyze various forms of data and glean from it what was factual and what was not. In this capacity, he became one of the most recognized and trusted employees in the FAA, often receiving formal recognition for his knowledge and integrity several times each year. As one Washington official said, "Cal has the courage to say what others are only thinking." He has brought that honesty to this book. Calvin retired in 1991 and now lives on a small ranch near Kansas City where he and his wife raise Angus cattle.

When he was twenty-one years old Calvin visited a church with a friend. It was a watershed event in his life. He saw a young woman and fell madly in love.

He says, "I would have married her the minute she said 'hello.' But it took almost seven years before she agreed to do it. I think she just decided I was going on her honeymoon anyway so she might as well take me along as her husband." Almost fifty years later, he is still madly in love with Delores, whom he affectionately calls "Sug." They have three sons and six grandchildren whom they adore—and daughters-in-law who became their own. "Family," says Cal, "is second only to God. But if you have God you also have family."

Calvin gave his life to Christ at age twenty-one and immediately began an intensive program to become the best Christian, preacher and teacher he could be. By the time he was thirty-five, he had memorized the entire New Testament, the Pentateuch, and several other books of the Old Testament. To build on that knowledge, he then turned his attention to an in-depth program of Biblical study. This book is the result of intensive research for the last six of those years.

Serving as an elder or minister for almost fifty years, Calvin has preached and taught over four thousand lessons. He and his wife, Delores, have also made monetary contributions to individuals, churches and missions throughout the world. As they say, "We may not have much money but we sure have good memories."

Calvin was often involved in community events, including two years as President and Board Chairman of the American Cancer Society of Kansas City and Public Relations Director for the Combined Federal Campaign. He was also recognized both by his employer, the Federal Aviation Administration, receiving their highest award, and the NAACP for advancing the cause of those who have suffered because of prejudice.

There are not many "Cal" Fields! In an age where human and civil rights of all kinds are high fashion, he plowed that ground decades ago, often to his detriment. He has always put God, family, country and his human obligation first. That is no small matter, especially in an era of human selfishness.

As a preacher and teacher, Calvin has always delivered powerful, thought-provoking presentations that were spiritually and doctrinally sound. Now he has embarked on a new adventure in his life—writing. This is extremely exciting because he will now be able to have an impact on countless individuals in their quest for scholarship and eternal life for generations to come. This book is a must read for people of all faiths and accomplishments, both religious and scientific.

Tom McMorris, B.S., M.S., Ed.S.
Sylvia McMorris, R.N., Ed.S.

Knowledge is the antidote to fear.

Ralph Waldo Emerson

PROLOGUE

THINGS YOU MAY HAVE NEVER HEARD IN BIBLE CLASS OR FROM THE pulpit, about the Bible and creation, are in this book. The confessions of evolutionists that you may have never heard about in the media and are hush-hush in the classroom—either illegal by state law or **forbidden by a conspiracy of silence!**—are also revealed in this book. The last six years of my life have been devoted to these discoveries.

It is not that I have any claim to fame or "name" recognition—no doctorates in either science or religion. But I do have an inquisitive mind and, as a professional analyst, a lifetime of education and experience separating fact from subjective speculation. Of most importance to the reader, what I have written is a **short "critical review" of competing issues** which have been written about in great detail in other books—books, including the Bible, about God, about Christ, about creation, and about evolution.

Such books have their place and without them I could not have written this book. I am deeply and gratefully thankful to their authors and research teams. But most of these works are lengthy, generally containing several hundred pages on just one subject. As such, they are highly technical and often presented in words and phrases rarely used in everyday conversation. They are mostly written by and for other scholars. **This book is written for everyday people!**

But any book of this nature, regardless of the audience, requires a high level of diligence on the part of the reader. For it deals with subjects on which there are endless and often deeply imbedded opinions. It challenges readers to examine what is presented with a mind open to new ideas and to have the strength of will to make changes, when warranted, in their belief systems. As Seneca, a Roman philosopher once said, "The mind is slow in unlearning what it has been long in learning."

Because of this inherent obstacle to learning, I urge each reader to use this book as a stepping stone to a deeper and richer study of the subjects covered. I especially recommend those books from which I have quoted—both those that would lend support and those that would disagree with my conclusions. It is always important to hear "what the other fellow has to say" (Proverbs 18:17).

I have tried to present, in a brief and hopefully understandable way, strong and compelling evidence that the Bible is from God and that Jesus Christ is the Son of God and Savior of the world. The reader can determine from the evidence presented whether or not this is just another religious proclamation or something derived from logic and reason. But if what is presented is true, then all other religious belief systems must be from men and not God. I know this is an emotional trigger, that it is not "politically correct" to say such a thing, but it is an oxymoron to profess belief that Christ is who He claimed to be and accord equal credibility to any other belief system. Jesus made this clear when He said, **"I am the way and the truth and the life. No one comes to the Father except through me"** (John 14:6). And the great Apostle Peter said, **"Salvation is found in no one else,** for there is no other name under heaven given to men by which we must be saved" (Acts 4:12). Another writer expressed this in a more stark and dramatic way:

> *Anyone who rejected the Law of Moses died without mercy on the testimony of two or three witnesses. How much more severely do you think a man deserves to be punished who has trampled the Son of God under foot, who has treated as an unholy thing the blood of the covenant that sanctified him, and who has insulted the Spirit of grace? For we know him who said, "It is mine to avenge; I will repay," and again, "The Lord will judge his people." It is a dreadful thing to fall into the hands of the living God* (Hebrews 10:28-31).

Aside from presenting what I believe to be compelling evidence that Christ is the Savior of the world, I have included equally compelling evidence that unrestricted organic evolution is long on rhetoric and short on substance. **By admission of its own adherents**, the fossil evidence essential to Darwinian theories, and which he predicted future scientists would find, has not been found! If, then, it has not been found, where is the evidence for commonly accepted evolutionary theories? Is it possible that these theories survive only through politically correct "words" where truth is sacrificed to self-imposed and limiting paradigms? These paradigms rule and control thought processes as much as any religious doctrine whereby philosophical ideologies assume worshipful proportions and become intellectual Gods.

The fallacy of these theories is not exposed by me or any other religious writer, for we are not scientists, but by testimony of some of the world's leading paleontologists, anthropologists, biologists and others in the scientific community. Anyone can verify the accuracy of this statement by spending some time at the public library reading books written by or about these scientists. But in fairness, whenever using quotations by these men and women, I have tried to avoid misrepresenting the underlying beliefs by most of them that evolution is a better theory than the most common interpretations of the Bible's account of supernatural creation. I sincerely apologize if I fail that task in some respect.

It is fair to say that all evolutionists reject a literal interpretation of the first chapter of Genesis. It is unfair to say that all evolutionists reject God and the reality and mission of Jesus Christ. Many are very forthcoming in their religious beliefs. But regardless of what they do or do not believe about God, it is by their own words, not mine, that the shortcomings of Darwinian theories become apparent. Theories that, by intent or not, provide a breeding ground for racism and other forms of physical and mental discrimination. It is by no means the only reason for this moral outrage but, as you will soon see, it certainly ranks as one of the major culprits.

A third theme of this book deals with the Biblical account of creation—what the Bible says and, perhaps more importantly, what it does not say. My objective, then, is not to provide detailed answers to all questions, **which I do not have**, but rather supply each reader with sufficient thought-provoking questions and observations as to allow for a reasonable correlation of the Biblical account of creation with geological, archaeological and fossil records—including fossil and archaeological records that show modern humans to be an amazingly unique and recent arrival in the chain of earth's long history.

May God bless this work! It represents what I have learned from numerous books, articles, tapes, speeches and personal studies over the last fifty years. Hopefully, it is sufficiently succinct and understandable to allow you, the reader, to comprehend what is at stake—your soul—your eternal destiny! For when the cold hand of death comes to touch you and the sugarcoated sayings of philosophers have melted away, what will you be thinking? When evolutionary theories that diminish God have run out of time and all human knowledge no longer gives comfort and hope, what will you be thinking? And when all your worldly goods and personal achievements no longer have any meaning, what will you be thinking? Jesus put these questions in stark, cold perspective:

What good will it be for a man if he gains the whole world, yet forfeits his soul? Or what can a man give in exchange for his soul? (Matthew 16:26).

We did not follow cleverly invented stories when we told you about the power and coming of our Lord Jesus Christ, but we were eyewitnesses of his majesty.

2 Peter 1:16

CHAPTER ONE

The Bible and Jesus Christ

THERE ARE MANY WELL-KNOWN RELIGIOUS BELIEFS IN THE WORLD. Most teach the value of human virtue. No religion has the market on decent, kind and honorable people. Because of this, every thoughtful person has the moral obligation to protect, even to the ultimate sacrifice, the right of each person to worship God according to the dictates of his or her conscience. We may disagree with our neighbors about their religion but should treat them with the utmost respect and courtesy. Hate-mongering groups or individuals that profess to be Christians make a mockery of Jesus' rules for Christian conduct:

> You have heard that it was said, "Eye for eye, and tooth for tooth." But I tell you, "Do not resist an evil person. If someone strikes you on the right cheek, turn to him the other also. And if someone wants to sue you and take your tunic, let him have your cloak as well. If someone forces you to go one mile, go with him two miles. Give to the one who asks you, and do not turn away from the one who wants to borrow from you." You have heard that it was said, "Love your neighbor and

*hate your enemy." But I tell you, "Love your enemies and pray for those who persecute you, that you may be sons of your Father in heaven. He causes his sun to rise on the evil and the good, and sends rain on the righteous and the unrighteous. If you love those who love you, what reward will you get? Are not even the tax collectors doing that? And **if you greet only your brothers, what are you doing more than others?** Do not even pagans do that? Be perfect, therefore, as your heavenly Father is perfect"* (Matthew 5:38-48).

Though I strongly believe in and respect the right of each person to worship as his or her conscience dictates, I have an equally strong conviction that the Christian religion has a lot more to offer than any other system of belief. For the Bible, which reveals Christian doctrine, also reveals the only true and living God. Were it not for ancient Biblical prophecies and their fulfillment in Jesus Christ, it would be difficult to make such a statement. It is in the fulfillment of these prophecies that we find a humanly impossible series of events that provide overwhelming evidence that the Bible is true and that Jesus Christ is the Son of God.

But remove Christ from the Bible and we are left with a set of religious laws, even though given by God to the Jewish nation, that violate our modern sense of mercy and impose upon us an impossible burden. As the Apostle Peter said, when referring to the ancient laws of the Old Testament, "Why do you try to test God by putting on the necks of the disciples a yoke that neither we nor our fathers have been able to bear? No! We believe it is through the grace of our Lord Jesus that we are saved" (Acts 15:10-11). And the Apostle John said, "For the law was given through Moses; **grace and truth came through Jesus Christ**" (John 1:17).

The Bible, without the mercy and kindness found in the New Testament of Jesus Christ, mandates the execution, most often by stoning, of those convicted of adultery, homosexuality, cursing father or mother, teaching another religious doctrine, or fortune-telling (Leviticus 20:9-16, 27; 24:14). It even demands death by stoning for those who work on the Sabbath (Numbers 15:32-35). Jesus drew a stark contrast between strict adherence to laws of the Old Testament and the illuminating grace of their intent in the New Testament:

One Sabbath Jesus was going through the grain fields, and as his disciples walked along, they began to pick some heads of grain. The Pharisees said to him, "Look, why are they doing what is unlawful on the Sabbath?" He answered, "Have you never read what David did when he and his companions were hungry and in need? In the days of Abiathar the high priest, he entered the house of God and ate the consecrated bread, which is lawful only for priests to eat. And he also gave some to his companions." Then he said to them, "The Sabbath was made for man, not man for the Sabbath" (Mark 2:23-28).

He went into the synagogue, and a man with a shriveled hand was there. Some of them were looking for a reason to accuse Jesus, so they watched him closely to see if he would heal him on the Sabbath. Jesus said to the man with the shriveled hand, "Stand up in front of everyone." Then Jesus asked them, "Which is lawful on the Sabbath: to do good or to do evil, to save life or to kill?" But they remained silent. He looked around at them in anger and, **deeply distressed at their stubborn hearts**, *said to the man, "Stretch out your hand." He stretched it out, and his hand was completely restored. Then the Pharisees went out and began to plot with the Herodians how they might kill Jesus* (Mark 3:1-6).

So in everything, do to others what you would have them do to you, for this sums up the Law and the Prophets (Matthew 7:12).

Love your enemies, do good to those who hate you, bless those who curse you, pray for those who mistreat you (Luke 6:27-28).

When they came to the place called the Skull, there they crucified him, along with the criminals—one on his right, the other on his left. Jesus said, "Father, forgive them, for they do not know what they are doing" (Luke 23:33-34).

Compare such teachings and actions of Christ with Islamic fundamentalists who are dedicated to the elimination of opposing doctrines by any necessary means. "Islam's Shari'a laws, derived from the Koran and sometimes part of the legal code,'are used to invoke discrimination, repression and out-right persecution against Christians'" (Peter Marshall, *Their Blood Cries Out*).

But why should this surprise anyone? The shoe has often been on the other foot. How many times have those who profess to be Christians persecuted Moslems, Jews and even each other, such as the countless conflicts between Catholics and Protestants? Or "ethnic cleansing" in the name of Christ? Or the cloak of religion used by colonialists to steal from and abuse other people, including the Indian nations of our own country? Or a burning cross, used by the Ku Klux Klan, as a symbol of hate?

Such hatred and discrimination is the height of hypocrisy. Jesus, founder of the Christian religion, is called "The Prince of Peace" (Isaiah 9:6). The very essence of His teaching is captured in the command, "Do not be overcome by evil, but overcome evil with good" (Romans 12:21). But aside from the unmatched morality of Christian doctrine, there is something about its author that makes it unique among all the religions of the world—**its founder claimed to be the Son of God**:

> *As soon as the chief priests and their officials saw him, they shouted, "Crucify! Crucify!" But Pilate answered, "You take him and crucify him. As for me, I find no basis for a charge against him." The Jews insisted, "We have a law, and according to that law he must die, because he claimed to be the Son of God"* (John 19:6-7).

What an incredible claim! If it's true, then every person on earth is faced with a reality about religious beliefs that demand a personal introspection. But if it's not true, then Jesus Christ is a fraud and Christianity nothing more than any other religious invention of the human mind.

But before we go any further a clarification needs to be made about the "Jews," a word often used in the Bible when referring to the enemies of Christ. It is very important we understand what is meant. Many have used this as a basis for anti-Semitism. What an incredible and ignorant misapplication of Scripture! Christianity itself is a Jewish religion! The very books of the Bible that refer to the enemies of Christ as "Jews" **were written by "Jews"**! The terminology had absolutely nothing to do with their physical identity. It was strictly a spiritual matter, used only by Bible writers to identify those Jews, their "brothers," who opposed the teachings of Christ:

I speak the truth in Christ—I am not lying, my conscience confirms it in the Holy Spirit—I have great sorrow and unceasing anguish in my heart. For I could wish that I myself were cursed and cut off from Christ for the sake of my brothers, those of my own race, the people of Israel... [for] my heart's desire and prayer to God for the Israelites is that they may be saved. For I can testify about them that they are zealous for God, but their zeal is not based on knowledge. Since they did not know the righteousness that comes from God and sought to establish their own, they did not submit to God's righteousness (Romans 9:1-5).

Even Jews who are not Christians are a special people. They are the physical children of Abraham, Isaac and Jacob. Based on our modern understanding of genetics, I know that whenever I touch my Jewish friends I am literally touching the patriarchs, maybe even a descendant of one of the brothers of Jesus. Anyone who doubts that the Jews retain a special place in the mind of God should read Romans 11:22-29. A Jew is and shall ever remain a descendant of Abraham, "God's friend" (James 2:23). In God's sight, Jewish acceptance of Christ is the noblest thing they will ever do. They gain the grace of Christ and still remain "Jews," the only people on earth who can claim both a spiritual and physical relationship with Jesus. It would be a tragedy for all of us if most of their culture and traditions were discarded. They are living testimony of the goodness and severity of God.

We must never forget that Jesus Himself was a Jew. For several years all of His followers were Jews. In the time of Christ only a small number of Jews were the enemies of Christ, most of whom were powerful religious leaders and outspoken members of two religious groups, the Sadducees and Pharisees. The Jewish "people" held Christ in high esteem:

When the chief priests and the Pharisees heard Jesus' parables, they knew he was talking about them. They looked for a way to arrest him, but they were afraid of the crowd because the people held that he was a prophet (Matthew 21:46).

The real question, for Jews and Gentiles alike, is whether or not Jesus really was the anticipated Messiah, the Savior. To answer this question, all we have to do is apply the same rules of evidence we would to any other matter. If we do, there is every reason to expect the same conclusion as that reached by Simon Greenleaf, a Harvard University law professor, especially when we consider that Mr. Greenleaf was one of the greatest legal experts on the subject of evidence the world has ever known and author of American Law, The Formative Years. Not only has the Supreme Court of the United States cited this book, but the London Law Journal concluded that its author knew more about the laws of evidence than "all the lawyers who adorn the courts of Europe."[1] Here is how Mr. Greenleaf would use "evidence" to settle a disputed issue:

> The word Evidence, in legal acceptation, includes all the means, by which any alleged matter of fact, the truth of which is submitted to investigation, is established or disproved ... The true question, therefore, in trials of fact, is not, whether it is possible, that the testimony may be false, but whether there is sufficient probability of its truth; that is, whether the facts are proved by competent and satisfactory evidence (American Law, The Formative Years).

Using this legal criterion, is there "sufficient probability" that Jesus Christ is the Son of God? Does "competent and satisfactory evidence" exist? Professor Greenleaf, this internationally acclaimed jurist, did not think so—that is, until he was challenged by a student to apply his own rules of evidence to those claims. Then what did he think? This Jewish professor became a believer! Irrational and implausible statements did not convince Professor Greenleaf. He was convinced by objective and undeniable prophetical, historical and archaeological evidence. As you are about to learn, such evidence is too strong to dismiss.

Lee Strobel, a journalist, wrote a small book about his conversion to Christ entitled Inside The Mind Of Unchurched Harry and Mary. This man, like Mr. Greenleaf, started out a skeptic and became a devout believer. Mr. Strobel thought Jesus' claims and the Bible nothing more than human inventions. But his journalistic mentality pushed him to put those claims to the test. As reported in his book, he found, among many other things,

---

1. Irwin H. Linton, A Lawyer Examines the Bible (Grand Rapids, Mich.: Baker, 1943), page 36.

that a British journalist and lawyer, by the name of Frank Morrison, had set out to write a book exposing the resurrection of Christ as a myth. However, after careful study of the evidence, Mr. Morrison also turned to Christ.[2]

Mr. Strobel went further. He found that a scientist named Peter Stoner put the Bible to the ultimate test—the test of mathematics. Along with six hundred students, he calculated the probability of just eight of the Jewish prophecies about Jesus being fulfilled in any one person. It was less than one chance in one hundred quadrillion. Then Professor Stoner applied the same mathematical test to forty-eight of the Bible's prophecies. The result was one chance in 10 to the 157th power.[3] This is how Mr. Strobel reacted to such astronomical numbers:

> *I did some research and learned that atoms are so small that it takes a million of them lined up to equal the width of a human hair. I also interviewed scientists about their estimate of the number of atoms in the entire universe. I concluded that the odds of forty-eight Old Testament prophecies coming true in any one individual are the same as a person randomly finding a single predetermined atom among all the atoms in a trillion trillion trillion trillion billion universes the size of our universe!* (Lee Strobel, *Inside the Mind of Unchurched Harry and Mary*; Copyright 1993; Zondervan Publishing House, Grand Rapids, Michigan; page 37).

Consider the realistic impossibility of just a few of these prophecies being the invention of any one prophet. Then consider that there was not just one prophet but many—strangers from each other that lived hundreds of years apart. And then consider the impossible task Jesus would have had in getting many others, even his enemies—the Jewish leadership and Roman government—to make sure it all happened exactly as prophesied. It would be a virtual mathematical impossibility, especially for a man who grew up and lived in a remote country village, who was limited in formal education, and who never traveled more than a few miles from home—a

---

2. Irwin H. Linton, *A Lawyer Examines the Bible* (Grand Rapids, Mich.: Baker, 1943), page 36.
3. Peter W. Stoner, *Science Speaks* (Chicago: Moody Press, 1969), page 107.

carpenter who, by our standards, was a poor man, living well below the poverty level. With these things in mind, look at the scope and even the minutia of some of these prophecies:

PROPHECIES	MADE	FULFILLED
Descendant of Abraham	Gen 12:3 (1921 B.C.)	Matt 1:1
Descendant of Isaac	Gen 17:19 (1898 B.C.)	Matt 1:2
Descendant of Judah	Gen 49:10 (1689 B.C.)	Matt 1:3
Descendant of David	2 Sam 7:12-17 (1000 B.C.)	Matt 1:1
Place of his birth	Micah 5:2 (700 B.C.)	Matt 2:4-6
Slaughter of infants	Jer 31:15 (596 B.C.)	Matt 2:16-18
He would be a prophet	Deut 18:15-18 (1410 B.C.)	Acts 3:22-23
Deaf hear and blind see	Isaiah 29:18-19 (730 B.C.)	Matt 11:4-5
Spoke in parables	Psalm 78:2	Matt 13:34-35
Hated without reason	Psalm 35:19	John 15:24-25
Betrayed by a friend	Psalm 41:9	Luke 22:47-48
Sold—thirty pieces of silver	Zech 11:12-13 (487 B.C.)	Matt 26:14-15
Money used to buy potter's field	Zech 11:13 (487 B.C.)	Matt 27:1-10
Abandoned by friends	Psalm 38:11	Mark 14:49-50
Accused by false witnesses	Psalm 27:12	Matt 26:60-61
Silent when accused	Isaiah 53:7 (690 B.C.)	Matt 27:11-14
Crucified with criminals	Isaiah 53:12 (690 B.C.)	Luke 23:32-33
Cursed on tree (cross)	Deut 21:13 (1410 B.C.)	Galatians 3:13
Hands and feet pierced	Psalm 22:16	John 20:24-28
Sun darkened at noon	Amos 8:9 (760 B.C.)	Matt 27:45
Mocked and insulted	Psalm 22:7-8	Matt 27:39-43
Gall and vinegar to drink	Psalm 69:21	Matt 27:34-38
Cast lots for His coat	Psalm 22:18	John 19:24
No bones were broken	Psalm 34:20	John 19:32-36
His body pierced	Zech 12:10 (487 B.C.)	John 19:32-36
Buried with the rich	Isaiah 53:9 (690 B.C.)	Matt 27:57-60
Resurrected from death	Psalm 16:8-10	Luke 24:1-46
	Psalm 49:15	I Cor 15:18

‣ Date of prophecies are reasonable estimates.
‣ Psalm prophecies were probably made after 1000 B.C.

These and many other prophecies, **taken as a whole**, cannot be logically assigned to any figure in history except Jesus Christ. No one else even comes close! He alone is the embodiment of all the very best of human virtues these ancient prophets could assign to a future King, Judge and Priest. It is true that some of these prophecies also applied to human events more immediate to the time they were made. But it is also true that even these, in part or in whole, are also assigned a secondary meaning that refers to the promised Messiah of the Jewish people. Regardless of how a particular prophecy may be classified, it was still the interpretation and expectation of the Jewish people, their spiritual leaders and even people of other nations, that most of them referred to the coming Messiah:

> **Matthew 2:1-6:** *After Jesus was born in Bethlehem in Judea, during the time of King Herod, Magi from the east came to Jerusalem and asked, "Where is the one who has been born king of the Jews? We saw his star in the east and have come to worship him." When King Herod heard this he was disturbed, and all Jerusalem with him. When he had called together all the people's chief priests and teachers of the law, he asked them where the Christ was to be born. "In Bethlehem in Judea," they replied, "for this is what the prophet has written": But you, Bethlehem, in the land of Judah, are by no means least among the rulers of Judah; for out of you will come a ruler who will be the shepherd of my people Israel.*

> **Luke 2:25-33:** *Now there was a man in Jerusalem called Simeon, who was righteous and devout. He was waiting for the consolation of Israel, and the Holy Spirit was upon him. It had been revealed to him by the Holy Spirit that he would not die before he had seen the Lord's Christ. Moved by the Spirit, he went into the temple courts. When the parents brought in the child Jesus to do for him what the custom of the Law required, Simeon took him in his arms and praised God, saying: Sovereign Lord, as you have promised, you now dismiss your servant in peace. For my eyes have seen your salvation, which you have prepared in the sight of all people, a light for revelation to the Gentiles and for glory to your people Israel.*

John 1:40-42: Andrew, Simon Peter's brother, was one of the two who heard what John had said and who had followed Jesus. The first thing Andrew did was to find his brother Simon and tell him, "We have found the Messiah" (that is, the Christ). And he brought him to Jesus.

In the above examples, the prophecy about the birthplace of Christ is found in Micah 5:2 and is representative of many prophecies that, in the opinion of most Bible scholars, could not reasonably be applied to any historical figure except Christ. In addition to the identification of a town from which no future earthly king or judge arose, the verse concludes with another qualification that no person, **other than Christ**, could have met:

But you, Bethlehem Ephrathah, though you are small among the clans of Judah, out of you will come for me one who will be ruler over Israel, whose origins are from of old, from ancient times.

Who but Christ "was with God in the beginning" (John 1:2), whose "origins are from old, from ancient[4] times"? Even the Jewish scholars, whom Herod consulted, understood this prophecy applied to a future ruler of the Jews. So also did the non-Jewish "wise men" who, when they saw the new "star," began a long, difficult, dangerous and expensive journey to "worship him." There was no doubt in their minds that this Scripture had been fulfilled. **No other person, up to that time or since, has been identified as the "king of the Jews."** Nor is it likely there will ever be a future Jewish "king" arise in the democratic state of Israel, much less from the city of Bethlehem by one who could trace his roots back to King David. The "evidence" is all on the side of Christ.

An example of a prophecy that had an earlier fulfillment in a predecessor of Christ and a secondary and more important fulfillment in Christ is found in 2 Samuel 7:4-17. Of this prophecy, Matthew Henry said:

Some of these promises [in 2 Samuel 7:14-17] relate to Solomon, his [King David] immediate successor, and to the royal line of Judah.

---

4. While some contend this can also apply to a previous period of human history, the structure of the sentence is so much in favor of something beyond this that most other respected translations use the words "everlasting" or "eternity."

Others of them relate to Christ, who is often called...Son of David to whom these promises pointed and in whom they had their full accomplishment. He was of the seed of David, Acts 13:23. To him God gave the throne of his father David (Luke 1:32), all power both in heaven and earth, and authority to execute judgment. He was to build the gospel temple, a house for God's name, Zechariah 6:12-13. That promise, I will be his Father, and he shall be my Son, is expressly applied to Christ by the apostle, Hebrews 1:5. But the establishing of his house, and his throne, and his kingdom, forever (v. 13, and again, and a third time v. 16. forever), can be applied to no other than Christ and his kingdom. David's house and kingdom have long since come to an end; it is only the Messiah's kingdom that is everlasting, and of the increase of his government and peace there shall be no end (Matthew Henry's Commentary on the Whole Bible: New Modern Edition, Electronic Database. Copyright © 1991 by Hendrickson Publishers, Inc).

It was no secret that the Jewish scholars of that time, including those who were the enemies of Christ, interpreted this and many other related Scriptures to the coming Messiah; as did Josephus, a Jewish historian who lived in the time of Christ:

While the Pharisees were gathered together, Jesus asked them, "What do you think about the Christ? Whose son is he?" "The son of David," they replied. He said to them, "How is it then that David, speaking by the Spirit, calls him 'Lord'? For he says, 'The Lord said to my Lord: Sit at my right hand until I put your enemies under your feet.'" If then David calls him "Lord," how can he be his son? No one could say a word in reply, and from that day on no one dared to ask him any more questions (Matthew 22:41-46).

And when Pilate had condemned him to the cross at the instigation of our own leaders, those who had loved him from the first did not cease. For he appeared to them on the third day alive again, as the prophets had predicted and said many other wonderful things about him. And even now the race of Christians, so named after him, has not yet died out (Josephus, *Antiquities*, 18, 3. 3).

Whether Messianic prophecies were exclusively or secondarily applied to Christ was of little importance—both were accepted by Jewish and non-Jewish scholars alike. The rejection and crucifixion of Christ, at the instigation of Jewish leaders, was not because He failed to fulfill these prophecies, but because they saw in that fulfillment the loss of personal position, power and wealth. Ironically, blinded by human ambition, their own actions resulted in the ultimate fulfillment of these prophecies—the crucifixion and resurrection of Christ and establishment of the Christian religion, a radically different concept of religious life that focused on substance over pomp and ceremony.

Modern "scholars?" who would diminish the implication of these ancient prophecies in order to be "politically correct" would do well to consider what happened to these Jewish leaders. Less than fifty years after they rejected Christ they were killed or taken captive and the city of Jerusalem, including their temple, was reduced to rubble—an event Jesus predicted would happen:

> The days will come upon you when your enemies will build an embankment against you and encircle you and hem you in on every side. They will dash you to the ground, you and the children within your walls. They will not leave one stone on another, because you did not recognize the time of God's coming to you (Luke 19:43-44).

The above listing of prophecies that were fulfilled in Jesus, though not all inclusive, shows the numerous and varied events that were open to public scrutiny and could have been easily refuted by anyone living in Judea at the time of Christ, friend or foe. The ineffectiveness of Jewish scholars in debating with Jesus, whom they no doubt considered a country bumpkin from the small town of Nazareth, shows, in dramatic form, His identity as the Messiah, the Christ, the Son of God:

> While the Pharisees were gathered together, Jesus asked them, "What do you think about the Christ? Whose son is he?" "The son of David," they replied. He said to them, "How is it then that David, speaking by the Spirit, calls him Lord? For he says, 'The Lord said to my Lord: Sit at my right hand until I put your enemies under your feet.' If then

David calls him 'Lord,' how can he be his son?" No one could say a word in reply, and from that day on no one dared to ask him any more questions (Matthew 22:41-46).

Reason dictates that **Jesus' life, Jesus' death, and Jesus' resurrection are factual, historical events!** And if the contemporaries of Christ could not deny these things, by what line of reasoning could anyone challenge it today? From where or from whom could they obtain opposing evidence? In fact, critics of the accuracy of Biblical history have been consistently embarrassed as we learn more and more about these ancient people:

> *It may be stated categorically that no archaeological discovery has ever controverted a biblical reference. Scores of archaeological findings have been made that confirm in clear outline or in exact detail historical statements in the Bible* (Henry M. Morris, The Bible and Modern Science [Chicago: Moody, 1968], page 95).

An example of this is in fragments of the Gospel of Mark, found among the Dead Sea Scrolls, and dated just a few years after Jesus' death:

> *This is very important because it means Mark's record had to survive the acid test of any journalistic or historical writing—being published at a time when it could be read, criticized, and if inauthentic denounced by thousands of Jews, Christians, Romans, and Greeks who were living in Palestine at the time of Jesus ministry. That the early church chose Mark as one of the only four gospels (out of dozens in circulation) to be preserved for posterity in the New Testament also indicates the people closest to the events—Jesus' original followers— found Mark's report accurate and trustworthy; not myth, but true history* (Louis Cassels, United Press International, Nashville Banner, April 1, 1972).

Sir William Ramsay, Professor of Humanity, University of Aberdeen, Scotland, and an eminent archaeologist, did not originally believe in the authenticity of the book of Acts. For twenty-five years he tried to discredit it, believing it contained a lot of historical information that could be disproved through archaeology. If he could discredit the account he could discredit its author. This was extremely important since Luke, the author of Acts, also wrote one of the accounts about the birth, life, death and resurrection of Jesus Christ. Sir Ramsay surely knew the flip side of this approach. If he could not discredit Luke he would, to be honest with himself, have to acknowledge the accuracy of what this man wrote in his other book.

To Sir Ramsay's surprise, his findings confirmed the book of Acts as an amazingly reliable and meticulously accurate source of historical information. So much so that Sir Ramsay himself came to believe that Jesus Christ was, indeed, God's son, just as the Bible states.[5] He is not alone. A. N. Sherwin White, a respected historian at Oxford University in England, concluded that "any attempt to reject its basic historicity, even in matters of detail, is absurd" (A. N. Sherwin-White, *Roman Society and Roman Law in the New Testament* [Oxford: Clarendon Press, 1963], page 189).

Over the centuries, the Bible has withstood the test of critics whose theories have fallen by the wayside. The archaeologist's spade has proved the critics wrong and the Bible right. Many believed that David, the hero king of Israel, was nothing more than a Jewish legend. Archaeology has now debunked that criticism. For over a century there were those who doubted that King Solomon, David's son, had the "stables" of horses attributed to him. Then they found the remains of one of them. Even the Biblical attribution of Pontius Pilate as the governor of Judea has now been proved—again, through archaeological discovery.

There were even those who doubted that the Romans allowed relatives and friends to give a proper burial to anyone who was crucified. Of course, that was before archaeologists found a preserved skeleton, in a proper grave, of a young man who had been crucified in exactly the same manner as the Biblical account of Christ's crucifixion (John 19:31-42).

There are still many unresolved issues for those who are forever seeking to dismiss the Bible as a message from the one and only true God. But for the open-minded, there are simply too many issues of the past that have been resolved in favor of the Biblical account to dismiss it as anything but an amazingly accurate record of what actually happened. As such, one cannot logically dismiss its record of the life and death of Christ. Consider the

---

5. D. James Kennedy, *Why I Believe* (Dallas: Word, 1980), page 33.

following statement in the Bible about such an extraordinary and uncontested historical event that it can only be considered a sign from God:

> From the sixth hour until the ninth hour darkness came over all the land (Matthew 27:45).

Is there external evidence to support this Biblical account of darkness on the day Christ died? The best kind of evidence one could find. It was never challenged! Accepted as a fact that no one could deny. **There is not a single historical record that disputes the Biblical account!**

Apparently only one person even tried to formally explain it. His name was Thallus. He was born in Samaria, just north of where Christ was crucified. Although his writings have been lost to us, Julius Africanus, a Christian chronographer of the late second century, quoted from them and said, "Thallus, in his third book of histories, explains away this darkness as an eclipse of the sun."[6] But Thallus could not deny the darkness that occurred when Christ was crucified. **Everyone knew it happened!** He only sought to explain it away as a natural phenomenon, an eclipse of the sun.

Here's the problem with the explanation offered by Thallus. In fact, there are three insurmountable problems. First, even if it were an eclipse, how could the ancient prophet have been able to predict that Christ's crucifixion would occur at exactly the same time as a solar eclipse? **Only through the power and involvement of God!** The second problem adds an even greater dimension that reflects the involvement of God. An eclipse cannot occur during the full moon. And according to Julius Africanus there was a full moon at the time of Jesus' crucifixion.[7]

But the third problem is the most telling of all and reflects the extent to which someone will go to avoid acknowledging the occurrence of a supernatural event. Thallus said the darkness was due to a solar eclipse. Yet, even in his time, it was known that the darkness of a total solar eclipse **lasts only a few minutes!** The darkness when Jesus was crucified **lasted for three hours** (Matthew 27:45). Little wonder that no one else offered such an obviously absurd explanation. Or attempted any explanation at all.

---

6. F. F. Bruce, *The New Testament Documents*, Eerdmans, page 113.
7. Edward C. Wharton. *Christianity: A Clear Case of History*, Howard Publishing Co., page 7.

The darkness cannot be explained away as an ordinary act of nature. Then or now. It happened in an unnatural way! **The darkness screams across the ages as a sign from God!** Especially when we consider it was predicted to occur almost eight hundred years before Christ was crucified. A prophecy that predicted the very hour of the day when it was to take place (Amos 8:9). **It happened! Christ was real! His crucifixion was real! His resurrection was real!** C. J. Sharp used a statue to show how the Bible's sixty-six books, which contain these prophecies and their fulfillment in Jesus Christ, could only come from and through the power of God:

> *If a fragment of stone were found in Italy, another in Asia Minor, another in Greece, another in Egypt, and on and on until sixty six fragments had been found, and if when put together they fitted perfectly together, making a perfect statue of Venus de Milo, there is not an artist or scientist but would arrive immediately at the conclusion that there was originally a sculptor who conceived and carved the statue. The very lines and perfections would probably determine which of the great ancient artists carved the statue. Not only the unity of the Scriptures, but their lines of perfection, suggest One far above any human as the real author. That could be no one but God* (C. J. Sharp, *Why We Believe* [Cincinnati: Standard Publishing, 1932], pages 12-13).

Edward C. Wharton, in his book, *Christianity, A Clear Case of History,* presents a compelling and convincing case that both ancient and contemporary writers recognized Christ as a real and undeniable part of human history. A few excerpts from this book show the widespread acceptance of His reality:

> *Mara Bar-Serapion, in a letter to his son: "What advantage did the Athenians gain from putting Socrates to death? Famine and plague came upon them as a judgment for their crime. What advantage did the men of Samos gain from burning Pythagoras? In a moment their land was covered with sand. What advantage did the Jews gain from executing their king? It was just after that that their kingdom was abolished. God justly avenged these three wise men: the Athenians died of hunger; the Samians were overwhelmed by the seas; the Jews,*

ruined and driven from their land, live in complete dispersion. But Socrates did not die for good; he lived on in the teaching of Plato. Pythagoras did not die for good; he lived on in the statue of Hera. Nor did the wise King die for good; he lived on in the teaching which He had given" (British Museum Syriac Mss., F. F. Bruce, *Jesus and Christian Origins Outside the New Testament*, page 31).

Tacitus, born about A.D. *53, a highly regarded Roman historian, wrote: "Consequently, to get rid of the report, Nero fastened the guilt and inflicted the most exquisite tortures on a class hated for their abominations, called Christians by the populace. Christ, from whom the name had its origin, suffered the extreme penalty during the reign of Tiberous [sic] at the hands of one of our procurators, Pontius Pilatus"* (The Annals and the Histories, 15:44. From Britannica Great Books, vol. 15, page 168).

Suetonius, annalist and court official for Hadrian, from the Life of Claudius, about A.D. *120: "As the Jews were making constant disturbance at the instigation of Chrestus [Christ], he [Claudius] expelled them from Rome"* (Life of Claudius, 25:4). *It should be noted that Luke, the author of Acts, had recorded this incident about sixty years earlier (Acts 18:1-2).*

Although written from an opposing religious point of view, The Talmud, which deals with Jewish law, refers to "Yeshu'a [Jesus] of Nazareth." The Encyclopaedia Judaica (Jerusalem) acknowledges that the accounts by Matthew, Mark, Luke and John provided proof of his reality.

Josephus, Jewish Historian: "And there arose about this time Jesus, a wise man, if indeed we should call him a man; for he was a doer of marvelous deeds, a teacher of men who receive the truth with pleasure. He won over many Jews and also many Greeks. This man was the Messiah. And when Pilate had condemned him to the cross at the instigation of our own leaders, those who had loved him from the first did not cease. For he appeared to them on the third day alive again,

*as the prophets had predicted and said many other wonderful things
about him. And even now the race of Christians, so named after him,
has not yet died out" (Antiquities, 18, 3. 3).*[8]

F. F. Bruce, Christian historian: *"Whatever else may be thought of the
evidence from early Jewish and Gentile writers...it does at least establish, for those who refuse the witness of Christian writings, the historical character of Jesus himself. Some writers may toy with the fancy of
a Christ-myth, but they do not do so on the ground of historical evidence. The historicity of Christ is as axiomatic for an unbiased historian as the historicity of Julius Caesar. It is not historians who
propagate the 'Christ-myth' theories"* (F. F. Bruce, The New Testament
Documents, page 119).

H. G. Wells, eminent world historian, said it very succinctly, *"Here
was a man. This part of the tale could not have been invented"* (H. G.
Wells, The Outline of History, vol. 1, page 420).

The Apostles Paul and Peter, about whom the historian Luke wrote
extensively in the first century, gave the following summations regarding
the resurrection of Christ—summations that could have easily been
refuted by their enemies. This adversarial silence is historical acknowledgment of the reality of Christ and His resurrection from the dead:

*Now, brothers, I want to remind you of the gospel I preached to you,
which you received and on which you have taken your stand. By this
gospel you are saved, if you hold firmly to the word I preached to you.*

---

8. While some are critical of the accuracy of the writings of Josephus, such questioning should
forever be put to rest by a quotation from The Works of JOSEPHUS, translated by William
Whiston, A.M.: Hendrickson Publishers, 1987, page 815: "But before I produce the cita-
tions themselves out of Josephus, give me leave to prepare the reader's attention, by setting
down the sentiments of perhaps the most learned person and the most competent judge,
that ever was, as to the authority of Josephus, I mean of Joseph Scaliger, in the Prolegomena
to his book De Emendatione; Temporum, p. 17. 'Josephus is the most diligent and the greatest lover
of truth of all writers; nor are we afraid to affirm of him, that it is more safe to believe him, not only as
to the affairs of the Jews, but also as to those that are foreign to them, than all the Greek and Latin writers; and this, because his fidelity and his compass of learning are everywhere conspicuous.'"

Otherwise, you have believed in vain. For what I received I passed on to you as of first importance: that Christ died for our sins according to the Scriptures, that he was buried, that he was raised on the third day according to the Scriptures, and that he appeared to Peter, and then to the Twelve. After that, he appeared to more than five hundred of the brothers at the same time, most of whom are still living, though some have fallen asleep. Then he appeared to James, then to all the apostles, and last of all he appeared to me also...[for] We did not follow cleverly invented stories when we told you about the power and coming of our Lord Jesus Christ, but we were eyewitnesses of his majesty (1 Corinthians 15:1-8; 2 Peter 1:16).

Will Durant believed that if Christ were just an invention of the human mind it would be more of a miracle than healing the sick or opening the eyes of a blind man. His impact on humanity and morality is unmatched:

That a few simple men should in one generation have invented so powerful and appealing a personality, so lofty an ethic and so inspiring a vision of human brotherhood, would be a miracle far more incredible than any recorded in the Gospels...and that Jesus' life and teaching constitute the most fascinating feature in the history of Western man (Will Durant, *Caesar and Christ*, page 557).

Jesus Christ is the one and only connection with the one true God of the universe! By that truth we shall all be forgiven or judged:

Many have undertaken to draw up an account of the things that have been fulfilled among us, just as they were handed down to us by those who from the first were eyewitnesses and servants of the word. Therefore, since I myself have carefully investigated everything from the beginning, it seemed good also to me to write an orderly account for you, most excellent Theophilus, so that you may know the certainty of the things you have been taught. ...He told them, "This is what is written: 'The Christ will suffer and rise from the dead on the third day, and repentance and forgiveness of sins will be preached in his name to all nations, beginning at Jerusalem'" (Luke 1:1-4, 24:46-47).

God did this so that men would seek him and perhaps reach out for him and find him, though he is not far from each one of us. For in him we live and move and have our being. As some of your own poets have said, "We are his offspring." Therefore since we are God's offspring, we should not think that the divine being is like gold or silver or stone—an image made by man's design and skill. In the past God overlooked such ignorance, but now he commands all people everywhere to repent. For he has set a day when he will judge the world with justice by the man he has appointed. He has given proof of this to all men by raising him from the dead (Acts 17:27-31).

Therefore let all Israel be assured of this: God has made this Jesus, whom you crucified, both Lord and Christ. When the people heard this, they were cut to the heart and said to Peter and the other apostles, "Brothers, what shall we do?" Peter replied, "Repent and be baptized, every one of you, in the name of Jesus Christ for the forgiveness of your sins. And you will receive the gift of the Holy Spirit. The promise is for you and your children and for all who are far off—for all whom the Lord our God will call." With many other words he warned them; and he pleaded with them, "Save yourselves from this corrupt generation." Those who accepted his message were baptized, and about three thousand were added to their number that day (Acts 2:36-41).

Jesus Himself said, "I am the way and the truth and the life. No one comes to the Father except through me" (John 14:6). That's direct and unambiguous. All the "political correctness" in the world cannot change this reality anymore than the Roman soldiers could undo their terrifying mistake:

*When the centurion and those with him who were guarding Jesus saw the earthquake and all that had happened, they were terrified, and exclaimed, **"Surely he was the Son of God!"*** (Matthew 27:54).

Within the Bible itself there is such a continuity of purpose to the writings of so many different people, separated by time, distance and language, we cannot rationally dismiss them as coincidental. Neither can we dismiss the amount of overwhelming historical evidence that Jesus Christ is the Son of God. And while these Bible writings and other historical evidence may not satisfactorily answer all possible questions, a person would have to ignore both the laws of logic and legally accepted rules of evidence to dismiss their implications:

- **The Bible, which contains the prophecies about Jesus, must be a message from God.**
- **Jesus Christ, in whom the Biblical prophecies were fulfilled, must be the Son of God.**
- **History affirms the life, death and resurrection of Jesus Christ.**

To deny these conclusions is to also accuse the most decent and honorable man who ever lived of being a liar and a fraud. To say that Jesus was only a good man but not the Son of God, as He Himself claimed to be, is an oxymoron, a self-contradiction. Good men don't lie and deceive! Especially about something that puts their disciples in grave danger. Only Jesus, of all the religious objects men and women have worshipped, meets the test of "evidence" that He, and He alone, is the Savior of the world:

Salvation is found in no one else, for there is no other name under heaven given to men by which we must be saved (Acts 4:12).

Sadly, there are some Biblical scholars who not only reject this statement of exclusivity but also attribute much of what is written in the Bible about Jesus to the imagination or political inventiveness of early Christians. This was made quite apparent in an ABC program, narrated by Peter Jennings, June 26, 2000. Yet, the scholars interviewed on this program **could not cite a single source of evidence to support their speculations!** What they did was assume that Jesus was just an ordinary man, perhaps fathered illegitimately by a Roman soldier, and that the story of his miraculous conception was invented to take away the stigma of that relationship.

But this was not all. Many of these scholars also attributed the Biblical record of the miracles performed by Jesus to the imagination of Biblical writers. **Again, they could not cite one shred of evidence to support their statements!** More than one, however, said they based their conclusions on the fact that not all events in the life of Christ were recorded by all four Gospel writers, Matthew, Mark, Luke and John. That's incredible! I have read many books about the life of Abraham Lincoln. None of these works was a duplication of the other. Why? Because the target audience and personal writing styles dictated both the content and tone used by each writer. That is exactly why the differences exist in the Gospel accounts of the life of Jesus. Each writer was addressing his work to a different audience in his own peculiar style of writing. In fact, only a fraction, a tidbit, about the miracles and the life of Christ was written down at all:

> *Many have undertaken to draw up an account of the things that have been fulfilled among us, just as they were handed down to us by those who from the first were eyewitnesses and servants of the word* (Luke 1:1-2).

> *Jesus did many other miraculous signs in the presence of his disciples, which are not recorded in this book. But these are written that you may believe that Jesus is the Christ, the Son of God, and that by believing you may have life in his name...Jesus did many other things as well. If every one of them were written down, I suppose that even the whole world would not have room for the books that would be written* (John 20:30-31; 21:25).

After forcefully denying the accuracy of the Biblical record of these "eyewitnesses," to my utter amazement, as the program was drawing to a close, Mr. Jennings reported that most of these same scholars professed their belief in the resurrection of Christ from the dead. What an incredible statement! Jesus' birth was not miraculous! Jesus did not walk on the water, heal the sick, and raise the dead! But Jesus Himself was resurrected from the dead!

How, in the name of logic, could Jesus experience a miraculous resurrection from the dead but could not have also experienced a miraculous conception and been endowed with miraculous powers? Especially since the only way these scholars could know about the resurrection itself is from the very same Bible writers who also told us about the birth and life of Christ. Whenever I read or hear such "scholarly?" rebuffs to the authenticity of the Biblical record, a record derived from **eyewitnesses of impeccable character**, I thank God for old-fashioned logic.

This is what we speak, not in words taught us by human wisdom but in words taught by the Spirit, expressing spiritual truths in spiritual words.

1 Corinthians 2:13

CHAPTER TWO

The Bible Is a Spiritual Book

THE BIBLE IS NOT JUST ONE BOOK BUT SIXTY-SIX SEPARATE DOCU-
ments, written by over forty men, over a period of about sixteen hundred years.
It was written in the languages and cultural idioms of the people to whom or for
whom each document was addressed. Most of these documents, which are now
referred to as books and letters, are written in clear and unambiguous language,
even when they contain hyperbolic expressions. But many of these documents
also contain statements that are often difficult to understand—especially when
written in or interspersed with metaphorical signs and symbols, a linguistic
idiom whereby something that is commonly understood is used to represent
something else.

In spite of these difficulties in understanding some parts of the Bible,
the rule for successful living is to **read the Bible—every day!** Its lessons for
living cannot be improved upon. If followed by all people, abuse and intol-
erance of others would cease. There would be no such thing as war. Words
like thief, murderer, adulterer, child abuser, drunkard and divorcee would
be dropped from the languages of the world. Dads would be dads, moms

would be moms, and kids would be kids. And, believe it or not, even politicians would be respectful of each other. But this hasn't happened. The Bible itself states that only a "few" will read and obey it (Matthew 7:13-14). Sadly, throughout history, most men and women have chosen to disobey. One day, **judgment day**, they will face the consequences:

> *For although they knew God, they neither glorified him as God nor gave thanks to him, but their thinking became futile and their foolish hearts were darkened...Therefore God gave them over in the sinful desires of their hearts to sexual impurity for the degrading of their bodies with one another...Even their women exchanged natural relations for unnatural ones. In the same way the men also abandoned natural relations with women and were inflamed with lust for one another. Men committed indecent acts with other men, and received in themselves the due penalty for their perversion. Furthermore, since they did not think it worthwhile to retain the knowledge of God, he gave them over to a depraved mind, to do what ought not to be done. They have become filled with every kind of wickedness, evil, greed and depravity. They are full of envy, murder, strife, deceit and malice. They are gossips, slanderers, God-haters, insolent, arrogant and boastful; they invent ways of doing evil; they disobey their parents; they are senseless, faithless, heartless, ruthless. Although they know God's righteous decree that* **those who do such things deserve death***, they not only continue to do these very things but also* **approve of those who practice them** *(Romans 1:21-32).*

> *The acts of the sinful nature are obvious: sexual immorality, impurity and debauchery; idolatry and witchcraft; hatred, discord, jealousy, fits of rage, selfish ambition, dissensions, factions and envy; drunkenness, orgies, and the like. I warn you, as I did before, that* **those who live like this will not inherit the kingdom of God** *(Galatians 5:19-21).*

> *Woe to those who are wise in their own eyes and clever in their own sight. Woe to those who are heroes at drinking wine and champions at mixing drinks, who acquit the guilty for a bribe, but deny justice to the innocent. Therefore, as tongues of fire lick up straw and as dry*

*grass sinks down in the flames, so **their roots will decay and their
flowers blow away like dust;** for they have rejected the law of the
LORD Almighty and spurned the word of the Holy One of Israel*
(Isaiah 5:21-25).

*Anyone who rejected the law of Moses died without mercy on the tes-
timony of two or three witnesses. How much more severely do you
think a man deserves to be punished who has trampled the Son of
God under foot, who has treated as an unholy thing the blood of the
covenant that sanctified him, and who has insulted the Spirit of grace?
For we know him who said, "It is mine to avenge; I will repay," and
again, "The Lord will judge his people." **It is a dreadful thing to fall
into the hands of the living God*** (Hebrews 10:28-31).

The message is crystal clear. We must not only believe in Christ, we
must also acknowledge Him with deeds that provide a point of light for a
sin-darkened world, to "shine like stars in the universe" (Matthew 10:32-33;
Philippians 2:15). For "a person is justified by what he does and not by faith
alone" (James 2:24). Moreover, we must be sure that we do not "approve" of
those who live immoral and ungodly lives (Romans 1:32). Neither should we
participate in nor approve of **false doctrines that divide the people of God:**

*Not everyone who says to me, "Lord, Lord," will enter the king-
dom of heaven, but only he who does the will of my Father who is in
heaven. Many will say to me on that day, "Lord, Lord, did we not
prophesy in your name, and in your name drive out demons and per-
form many miracles?" Then I will tell them plainly, "I never knew
you. **Away from me, you evildoers!***" (Matthew 7:21-23).

*I appeal to you, brothers, in the name of our Lord Jesus Christ, that all
of you agree with one another so that there may be no divisions among
you and that you may be **perfectly united in mind and thought.** My
brothers, some from Chloe's household have informed me that there are
quarrels among you. What I mean is this: One of you says, "I follow
Paul"; another, "I follow Apollos"; another, "I follow Cephas"; still
another, "I follow Christ." **Is Christ divided?*** (1 Corinthians 1:10-13).

*I urge you, brothers, to **watch out for those who cause divisions and put obstacles in your way that are contrary to the teaching you have learned.** Keep away from them. For such people are not serving our Lord Christ, but their own appetites. By smooth talk and flattery they deceive the minds of naive people…**For such men are false apostles, deceitful workmen, masquerading as apostles of Christ.** And no wonder, for Satan himself masquerades as an angel of light. It is not surprising, then, if his servants masquerade as servants of righteousness. Their end will be what their actions deserve* (Romans 16:17-18; 2 Corinthians 11:13-15).

*For the time will come when men will not put up with sound doctrine. Instead, to suit their own desires, they will gather around them a great number of teachers to say what their itching ears want to hear. **They will turn their ears away from the truth and turn aside to myths*** (2 Timothy 4:3-4).

*My prayer is not for them alone. I pray also for those who will believe in me through their message, **that all of them may be one**, Father, just as you are in me and I am in you. May they also be in us so **that the world may believe that you have sent me*** (John 17:20-22).

Christ did not establish hundreds of different and competing churches. It is obvious that division among believers has been an enormous obstacle to the spread of Christianity and to the salvation of many people. It is extremely important that we not only avoid ungodly lifestyles, but **also avoid religious affiliations that are divisive and displeasing to God!** The only way to do that is by reading the Bible:

Study** to shew thyself approved unto God, a workman that needeth not to be ashamed, **rightly dividing the word of truth (2 Timothy 2:15, KJV).

In fact, everyone who wants to live a godly life in Christ Jesus will be persecuted, while evil men and impostors will go from bad to worse, deceiving and being deceived. But as for you, continue in what you *have learned and have become convinced of, because you know those from whom you learned it, and how from infancy you have known the holy Scriptures, which are able to make you wise for salvation through faith in Christ Jesus. All Scripture is God-breathed and is useful for teaching, rebuking, correcting and training in righteousness, **so that the man of God may be thoroughly equipped for every good work*** (2 Timothy 3:12-17).

The first and most important rule to remember, as we read the Bible, is that God's commands and spiritual principles for human conduct are easy to understand. This bears repeating. **God's commands and spiritual principles for human conduct are easy to understand!** But understanding and doing are two different things. Jesus said, "Honor your father and mother and love your neighbor as yourself" (Matthew 19:19). That's easy to understand. But how many of us actually do it? How many of us are willing to make the sacrifices of money and time to care for the elderly, even our own relatives, especially when they become a burden? Or go even further and try to justify disobedience by changing "the word of God for the sake of...tradition" (Matthew 15:3-9). In this example from Matthew, some of the Jewish leaders were trying to elevate tradition above the law of God so they would not have to take care of their parents. The Bible says that such people are "worse" than those who do not believe in God (1 Timothy 5:8).

Contrary to the very spirit of the Christian message, the Bible's great teachings have been distorted and changed in feeble attempts to justify abortion (murder), unauthorized divorce, sexual deviations and countless other sins of the flesh; and certainly not least is the desire to invent unauthorized religious doctrines. This is done in spite of the fact that **none of the great spiritual and moral teachings of the Bible are hidden from anyone** who seeks and "loves the truth" (1 Thessalonians 2:10). For those who "seek" will "find" (Matthew 7:7). Even when metaphors, cultural settings and linguistic idioms prevent us from understanding everything that is said, we can still grasp the **underlying principles** for Godly living.

It is deceptive for any Bible teacher to insist that everything in the Bible is crystal clear or that any one person has spiritual insight into all things. As every theologian knows, the Bible writers, from beginning to end, used linguistic idioms that have confused the most learned scholars.

This is why various interpretations have often been revised as new historical and scientific information became available:

> *But as to the fable that there are...men on the opposite side of the*
> *earth...is on no ground credible...For Scripture...gives no false infor-*
> *mation; and it is absurd to say, that some men might have taken ship*
> *and traversed the whole wide ocean, and crossed from this side of the*
> *world to the other, and that thus the inhabitants of that distant region*
> *are descended from that one man* (Augustine, The City of God, in Nicene
> and Post-Nicene Fathers, Eerdmans, Grand Rapids, 1956, volume 2, page 315).

We now know that the earth is round. But Augustine, a highly
respected fourth century theologian, who made the above statement,
thought such a notion "absurd." It has not been so long ago when this was
still being taught by many as a religious doctrine. To prove it adherents
quoted Revelation 7:1, "I saw four angels standing at the four-corners of the
earth." It was not until we learned that the earth really was round that theologians recognized this was a prophetical statement that had no reference
to the shape and configuration of the physical earth. Had they not been so
focused on the **linguistic license** used in one Scripture to the exclusion of
others such a religious doctrine would have never come into existence.
Isaiah 40:22 states that God "sits enthroned above the circle of the earth,"
which is hardly the description of a flat earth.

In the sixteenth century, Copernicus, an astronomer, said he believed
the earth rotated every twenty-four hours while orbiting the sun once each
year. Religionists were aghast that he would even suggest something so
obviously unscriptural. Martin Luther called him a "fool," stating that
"Joshua commanded the sun to stand still and not the earth."[9] We now
know that it was not Copernicus who was mistaken. It was not that the sun
literally stood still but only that it **appeared** to stand still, when viewed
from a human perspective. Again, **linguistic license!**

Perhaps most damaging to Biblical integrity was the famous Scopes
trial of 1925. It involved a Tennessee public school teacher, John Thomas

---

9. A. D. White, *A History of the Warfare of Science with Theology in Christendom*, 1896, repub-
lished Appleton, New York & London 1932, volume I, page 126.

Scopes, who explained the theory of evolution to his students. He was indicted for unlawfully teaching evolutionary theory. At that time, it was a crime in Tennessee as well as in many other states. For creationists, it provided an opportunity to put an end to evolutionary theories by proving the Bible was the only possible explanation for animal life.

William Jennings Bryan was chosen as the prosecutor. Bryan, an attorney, was also a former U.S. Secretary of State, respected journalist and an outstanding orator. He had been instrumental in persuading legislatures in many states to pass anti-evolution laws. The evolutionary forces, aided by the American Civil Liberties Union, chose Clarence Darrow and Dudley Field Malone to defend Scopes. For most people the issue was not about Scopes. It was about Darwin's theory of evolution and the freedom of speech.

Bryan was very persuasive. That is, until Darrow, for the defense, denied by the judge the use of expert witnesses, put Bryan himself on the stand. He felt his only option was to show that the Bible does not always require a literal interpretation. He attacked Bryan relentlessly with questions about the Genesis account of creation and other remarkable events recorded in the Bible. His aim was to have Bryan become confused and give conflicting testimony. It worked. Bryan finally admitted that some things recorded in the Bible should not be taken in a literal manner. Moreover, Bryan admitted he had no real knowledge about geology, physiology or archaeology. Nevertheless, Scopes lost. The judge had no choice. He had violated Tennessee law. He was fined one hundred dollars.

It was a hollow victory. Bryan was a poor witness for the Christian faith. Whatever his credentials as a lawyer and orator, he failed to prepare a logical correlation between the Bible and science—which, of course, was what people thought the trial was all about. But Bryan's most serious blunder was his failure to use the best evidence available, the fossil record, which had nothing to do with any particular religious doctrine. He could have shown that evolutionary naturalism, which will be discussed in a later chapter, **has no foundation in scientific fact!** Darrow, on the other hand, presented such a rational and logical defense that the public, **ignorant of the fossil record,** was persuaded there was nothing wrong with teaching the theory of evolution. In short, Darrow did his homework. Bryan did not.

By his inability to present a logical and rational case, based on scientific evidence instead of a religious document, Bryan not only publicly resurrected Darwinism but launched it into orbit and placed it in classrooms all across America. His repeated answer, "The Bible states it. It must be so," portrayed many Christians as bigoted and narrow-minded people who could not reconcile their faith with scientific findings. At the trial itself, when the attorney general wanted to know Darrow's real purpose in hammering away at Bryan, he received the following answer: "To prevent bigots and ignoramuses from controlling the educational system of the United States!"

As a result of this trial, augmented by highly biased and prejudiced plays and movies, such as the 1960 movie *Inherit The Wind*, based on the Scopes trial, many people now question the authenticity of the Bible itself—including a significant number of professing Christians who believe the Biblical account of creation to be mythological. What a distressing commentary on our educational systems, both church and public!

Throughout the ages, many religionists, like Augustine, Luther and Bryan, have encumbered their thinking process by taking everything in the Bible, a spiritual book, as being literal in everything that is said. This occurred because they failed to recognize that any infallibly correct religious doctrine must be credible and consistent with:

+ **All relevant Scriptures**
+ **Laws of the physical universe**
+ **Historical discoveries**

Two of the most significant causes of misunderstanding and disagreement about Bible passages are culture and language. Consider the statement often made within our own culture, "I've told you a hundred times to stop that." Or, "I'm gonna kill that kid." Sound familiar? These are just two of hundreds of hyperbolic or metaphorical statements used in current, everyday language. We understand the number is not literal, that the person has not been told a hundred times. We understand the mother is not going to literally kill her child. But would a person of another culture or language understand this? Especially when separated in time by thousands of years and with only, in many cases, minimal recorded history and archeological information to guide them? We have trouble understanding the language of the generation just behind us, much less that of a hundred generations ago. Further compounding the problem is the difficulty in translating ancient languages and sundry dialects that have not been used for thousands of years.

Another issue is the omission of details throughout the Bible, such as the complete lack of information as to why there are different races, colors and physical configurations of the human species. Was Adam tall or short? Was he hairy? Did he lose the hair on his head and become bald? Was he black or white or brown or yellow or some other color we don't even know about? And why did people before the Great Flood live so much longer than those born after the flood? And what did the first "kinds" of animals look like? Did God create saber-toothed tigers, lions and bobcats, or did he simply create a generic "kind" of animal that was the progenitor of all cats? Was it "all" done in a day, a year, or millions of years? And having fore-knowledge of our obsession with dinosaurs, why was God, through the Bible writers, silent about these awesome creatures?

Lack of such information, **this omission of details**, coupled with our modern **obsession** with filling in the blanks, has led to all kinds of specu-lation about creation—speculation that is often based more on religious emotion or political correctness than sound scientific data and Biblical teachings. Tragically, these **"opinions"** often become a test of Christian fel-lowship or unintentionally diminish the reality of a creative God.

Adding to this scenario is the fact that the Bible often employed Hebraic construction of words and phrases whereby **linguistic arrange-ments took precedence over accuracy!** An example is found in the first chapter of Matthew where the grouping of Christ's ancestors into blocks of "fourteen generations" was more important than inclusion of all their names. A similar approach was used by Moses when he gave the date when the firstborn son of Terah was born but substituted the name of Abraham, a younger son of more importance. Or that Cain had sexual relations with his wife when, if the Biblical sequence is taken literally, only he and his par-ents existed. Or the question of whether the sun, moon and stars were cre-ated on the first or fourth day.

But there is another factor of difficulty that goes beyond normal cul-tural and linguistic differences. The Bible itself, as mentioned earlier, often couches its teachings in words and phrases that are not always easy to understand, even by the people to whom the message is primarily addressed:

> *The knowledge of the secrets of the kingdom of God has been given to you, but to others I speak in parables, so that, though seeing, they may not see; though hearing, they may not understand* (Luke 8:10).

> *Then Philip ran up to the chariot and heard the man reading Isaiah the prophet. "Do you understand what you are reading?" Philip asked. "How can I," he said, "unless someone explains it to me?"* (Acts 8:30-31).

> *He writes the same way in all his letters, speaking in them of these matters. His letters contain some things that are hard to understand, which ignorant and unstable people distort, as they do the other Scriptures, to their own destruction* (2 Peter 3:16).

Why would God allow any part of the Bible to be so "hard to understand" that "ignorant and unstable people distort its teachings"? That's the wrong question! A more appropriate question would be, "Why do people deliberately distort commands of God that are not difficult to understand?" In other words, it would have made no difference. For we know that the key to understanding what God wants us to do is found in the content of our character and not in our difficulty in knowing how He wants us to live:

> *They perish because they **refused to love the truth** and so be saved. For this reason God sends them a powerful delusion so that they will believe the lie and so that all will be condemned who have not believed the truth but have delighted in wickedness* (2 Thessalonians 2:10-12).

> *In them is fulfilled the prophecy of Isaiah: "You will be ever hearing but never understanding; you will be ever seeing but never perceiving." **For this people's heart has become callused;** they hardly hear with their ears, and they have closed their eyes. Otherwise they might see with their eyes, hear with their ears, understand with their hearts*

and turn, and I would heal them. But blessed are your eyes because they see, and your ears because they hear (Matthew 13:13-16).

*We have not received the spirit of the world but the Spirit who is from God, that we may understand what God has freely given us. This is what we speak, not in words taught us by human wisdom but in words taught by the Spirit, **expressing spiritual truths in spiritual words**. The man without the Spirit does not accept the things that come from the Spirit of God, for they are foolishness to him, and **he cannot understand them**, because they are spiritually discerned* (1 Corinthians 2:12-14).

It is apparent that while the Bible is a book of truth, **it is a spiritual book** presented in the physical culture and linguistic idioms common to the ancient people to whom it was first addressed. Failure to understand this has often led people to some pretty drastic conclusions. A stark example of this occurred several years ago, in the author's own congregation, when a young man, believing the following Scripture was to be taken literally, took an ax and cut off his finger:

And if your right hand causes you to sin, cut it off and throw it away. It is better for you to lose one part of your body than for your whole body to go into hell (Matthew 5:30).

Did Jesus really tell him to cut off his finger? Would the finger go to Hell while the rest of the body went to Heaven? The action of this young man shocked the entire congregation. But why should it? Are we faultless in making Scripture literal in ways never intended by Bible writers? Countless people have wedded themselves to destructive beliefs by making literal those things that are nothing more than linguistic metaphors. Dangerous cults serve as prime examples. We should always keep in mind that using a figure of speech to demonstrate a spiritual principle occurs throughout the Bible and involves almost every subject imaginable:

And when you give to the needy, do not let your left hand know what your right hand is doing, so that your giving may be in secret (Matthew 6:3-4).

It would be mentally impossible to give in the manner illustrated by Jesus. Our mind always knows what each hand is doing. In another instance much ado has been made about two writers providing different details about the same event:

> I tell you the truth," Jesus answered, "this very night, before the rooster crows, you will disown me three times" (Matthew 26:34).

> Immediately the rooster crowed the second time. Then Peter remembered the word Jesus had spoken to him: "Before the rooster crows twice you will disown me three times." And he broke down and wept (Mark 14:72).

Did the rooster crow once or twice? Or did Mark simply provide more detail in marking the time? Either way, the crux of the event is not diminished—Peter would deny Christ before the night was out. In the case of the rooster two writers were involved, but in another instance a single author, in describing details about the same event, used similar linguistic freedom:

> The men traveling with Saul stood there speechless; they heard the sound but did not see anyone (Acts 9:7).

> My companions saw the light, but they did not understand the voice of him who was speaking to me (Acts 22:9).

In the first instance, Luke, author of the book of Acts, said they heard. In the second, he elaborated by saying they heard but did not understand. Both statements are correct. One simply provides more detail than the other. In fact, without benefit of the second Scripture, we would have incorrectly believed that Saul's companions also understood the voice. In this case, it would have had little or no influence on our belief systems. But Scripture isolation, that is, building a religious doctrine by ignoring related and clarifying Scriptures, has often led to serious doctrinal errors:

> The sun will be turned to darkness and the moon to blood before the coming of the great and glorious day of the Lord. And everyone who calls on the name of the Lord will be saved (Acts 2:20-21).

Not everyone who says to me, "Lord, Lord," will enter the kingdom of heaven, but only he who does the will of my Father who is in heaven (Matthew 7:21).

We know the moon did not turn to blood. Any serious Bible student knows this is symbolic language, a metaphor, depicting a great event in human affairs. But what about "everyone" who calls on God? Are they saved or not? Luke said they would be. Matthew said they would not. Can both be right? In Acts, the **context** shows that those who "call" on the Lord will also do His bidding. In Matthew, Jesus specifically states that calling Him "Lord" is not enough. In both cases the same thing is taught. There is no conflict. **Belief must be accompanied with obedience!** We must give up our will for **His will** (Romans 6:11-23). Disagreements can also develop because of our failure to respect minor translation inconsistencies, such as what each writer included or excluded about something as exacting as numbers:

With the two sons who had been born to Joseph in Egypt, the members of Jacob's family, which went to Egypt, were seventy in all (Genesis 46:27).

After this, Joseph sent for his father Jacob and his whole family, seventy-five in all (Acts 7:14).

Which number is correct? In the above text from Acts, Stephen, the speaker, may have quoted "seventy-five" from the Septuagint version, a translation into Greek from Hebrew prior to the time of Christ and one with which his audience was familiar. The Hebrew text available to us today shows that the number in Genesis is seventy, but we do not know which Hebrew texts were available to the Septuagint translators. No doubt many were lost when Amru, an Arab general, in A.D. 638, destroyed most of the library at Alexandria, Egypt, where the translation took place. But does this difference in numbers that have come down to us discredit the text, much less the entire Bible? Hardly! Either one identifies the point being made—from a few came a nation of millions. No one quibbled with Stephen about the numbers! But they killed him because of the content of his message about Christ (Acts 7:1-60). Another issue is the Hebrew language idiom regarding the reckoning of time:

> For as Jonah was three days and three nights in the belly of a huge fish, so the Son of Man will be three days and three nights in the heart of the earth (Matthew 12:40).

If Jesus was crucified on Friday afternoon and resurrected on Sunday morning, how could He have fulfilled this prophecy? He couldn't, by our method of reckoning time. But it posed no problem for the Jews of the first century:

> Many examples might be produced, from both the sacred and profane writers, in vindication of the propriety of the expression in the text...Thus, then, three days and three nights, according to this Jewish method of reckoning, included any part of the first day; the whole of the following night; the next day and its night; and any part of the succeeding or third day...this, no doubt, exactly corresponded to the time in which Jonah was in the belly of the fish.[10] Several days were usually reckoned by the Jews as inclusive of the parts of both extremes.[11] It is a manner of speech very usual.[12]

We find no historical example, religious or secular, that challenged Jesus' statement in light of what actually occurred. **For them**, it was linguistically correct. A similar reckoning is found in Acts 10:30 when Cornelius said, "Four days ago I was in my house praying." An analysis of the context, by our method of counting time, shows it to have been three days.

We also find it impossible, from the Bible, to know when the earth and its inhabitants were created, including Adam and Eve. Counting the generations of people who lived in the Bible won't work. The Bible abounds with evidence of generation gaps. Neither is the Bible crystal clear as to the length of each of the creative days (Genesis, chapter 1). There are many

---

10. *Adam Clarke Commentary.*
11. *Strong's Greek/Hebrew Dictionary.*
12. *Matthew Henry's Commentary.*

Christians who believe they were twenty-four hour solar days. Other Christians believe they were metaphors for indeterminate periods of time. Both groups include scientists of considerable reputation. The easy thing, of course, is to simply say that a day is a day. But, in the Bible, a day is not always just another day any more than a year is just a year:

> ***Ecclesiastes 6:3-6:*** *"...a stillborn child is better off than [a] man [who] lives a thousand years twice over but fails to enjoy his prosperity."* Obviously, "thousand" is nothing more than a linguistic idiom and has no reference to a specific period of time.

> ***Isaiah 65:2:*** *"All day long I have held out my hands to an obstinate people, who walk in ways not good, pursuing their own imaginations."* Again, this is a linguistic metaphor for an indeterminate period of time.

> ***Luke 13:32-33:*** *"I will drive out demons and heal people today and tomorrow, and on the third day I will reach my goal. In any case, I must keep going today and tomorrow and the next day—for surely no prophet can die outside Jerusalem!"* It was more than three literal days after this before Jesus was crucified.

> ***Revelation 12:6:*** *"The woman fled into the desert to a place prepared for her by God, where she might be taken care of for 1,260 days."* Many believe the "woman" is a metaphor for the Lord's Church and that the "1,260 days" represent 1,260 years.

> ***2 Peter 3:8:*** *"With the Lord a day is like a thousand years, and a thousand years are like a day."* Again, a metaphor illustrating that God is not bound by the limitations of a solar clock.

The foregoing serve only as examples of the many variables that show the necessity for observing the **context** in which a word or phrase appears, **or the degree to which other related Scriptures clarify its meaning!** The problems are further exacerbated if we use a Bible that was not translated by credible scholars. Translators must not only decipher the meaning of words but the **thought** expressed by the context and arrangement of the words. Each translator also uses his own unique style of expression. Moreover, some Greek and Hebrew texts are difficult to translate because of a lack of understanding of ancient cultures and language idioms. Even the manuscripts and many other writings used by the translators are not originals, but either handmade copies or translations from documents long since lost or destroyed by normal aging, natural disasters and overt attempts by the enemies of Christ to destroy all evidence of the Christian faith.

These factors virtually ensure that differences in words and sentence structure will vary among translators. No two will do it exactly the same— especially when confronted with the fact that even our own language is constantly changing. For example, the King James Version is an excellent and treasured translation. It is the one with which I am most familiar and most often quote in my sermons and lessons. But it is obvious to anyone that many of its words and phrases are outdated, quite different from modern English.

Yet, in spite of all these variables and theological rhetoric about minor differences of opinion concerning this or that translation, **the God of Heaven has preserved the essential content of the Scriptures!** Preserved to such an amazing degree that anyone, with a receptive mind, can find within all scholarly translations sufficient information to become a Christian and **live as God desires!**

Because we are blessed with the availability of so many good translations, we should certainly not waste our time and energy worrying that we do not have the "Word of God." **We do!** Neither should we be concerned about such things as the age of the earth or its inhabitants. We only need to put our common sense in gear and look up, around and down to know that none of this happened by accident. What we are to do, in fact commanded to do, is to avoid becoming entangled with the things of this world that have little or nothing to do with our relationship with God "which is by faith."

As I urged you when I went into Macedonia, stay there in Ephesus so that you may command certain men not to teach false doctrines any longer nor to devote themselves to myths and endless genealogies.

These promote controversies rather than God's work—which is by faith. The goal of this command is love, which comes from a pure heart and a good conscience and a sincere faith. Some have wandered away from these and turned to meaningless talk. They want to be teachers of the law, but they do not know what they are talking about…Have nothing to do with godless myths and old wives' tales; rather, **train yourself to be godly** (1 Timothy 1:3-7; 4:7).

No one serving as a soldier gets involved in civilian affairs—he wants to please his commanding officer. Similarly, if anyone competes as an athlete, he does not receive the victor's crown unless he competes according to the rules. The hardworking farmer should be the first to receive a share of the crops. Reflect on what I am saying, for the Lord will give you **insight** *into all this* (2 Timothy 2:4-7).

The "insight" to which the Bible refers is that our concentration, our primary focus in life, should be on those things that will testify as to the "content of our character" (Martin Luther King, Jr.). Insisting on having a detailed and literal answer to everything mentioned in the Bible, much less those areas of study where there is not enough information to determine an infallible religious doctrine, violates the very essence of these commands. Such as the fact that while the Bible, a spiritual book, contains many things about nature and historical events that attest to its divine authorship, it is not, and never was intended to be, a book about science, astronomy, medicine, or any other human discipline. It says nothing about space exploration, submarines, stock markets, automobiles, television, computers, DNA or a million other things of the modern world.

As previously discussed, failure to recognize the spiritual nature and limitations of the Bible has led religious people into some embarrassing doctrinal quagmires. Especially they fail to recognize that **whatever God reveals in nature is as credible as a statement from the Bible! He is the author of both!** For He, who "does not lie" (Titus 1:2), tells us in unmistakable language that "since the creation of the world God's invisible qualities—his eternal power and divine nature—have been clearly seen, **being understood from what has been made**" (Romans 1:20). Even the lowly ant has been endowed by God with natural attributes which, He tells us, by careful observation and application, can turn a "sluggard" into a "wise" and productive human being (Proverbs 6:6). But perhaps the best evidence that God expects us to learn from nature is found in the Book of Job:

> But ask the animals, and they will **teach** you, or the birds of the air, and they will **tell** you; or speak to the earth, and it will **teach** you, or let the fish of the sea **inform** you (Job 12:7-8).

It should be obvious by now that the Bible, though an inspired message, was written in a manner that reflected the historical setting, language, education, feelings and customs of people quite different from us. Included were idiomatic expressions that did not always represent literal events, numbers and relationships. That God dealt with these ancient people based on their level of understanding is also quite clear. Hardened hearts, plain old ignorance, and difficulty absorbing God's great teachings limited what He revealed:

> I have much more to say to you, more than you can now bear (John 16:12).

> We have much to say about this, but it is hard to explain because you are slow to learn (Hebrews 5:11).

> Bear in mind that our Lord's patience means salvation, just as our dear brother Paul also wrote you with the wisdom that God gave him. He writes the same way in all his letters, speaking in them of these matters. His letters contain some things that are hard to understand (2 Peter 3:15-16).

> Do your best to present yourself to God as one approved, a workman who does not need to be ashamed and who correctly handles the word of truth (2 Timothy 2:15).

> Study to shew thyself approved unto God, a workman that needeth not to be ashamed, rightly dividing the word of truth. (2 Timothy 2:15 KJV).

In fact, though by this time you ought to be teachers, you need some-one to teach you the elementary truths of God's word all over again. You need milk, not solid food! Anyone who lives on milk, being still an infant, is not acquainted with the teaching about righteousness. But solid food is for the mature, who by constant use have trained them-selves to distinguish good from evil (Hebrews 5:12-14).

One who "correctly handles" or is "rightly dividing" the Scriptures must always be amenable to enlightenment. We must never try to take those things that are cultural or couched in metaphors or obscure meanings and bind them as religious laws upon other people, especially those who are separated by thousands of years, different languages, and a vast level of knowledge. **So long as no fundamental principle of the Gospel is violated**, God expects Christians to adapt that Gospel to the cultural idiosyncrasies, and most assuredly advancements in knowledge, of the people being taught. It is one of the main differences between the law of Christ and religions that are more interested in tradition, form, and format than in love, mercy, and justice:

*To the Jews I became like a Jew, to win the Jews. To those under the law I became like one under the law...so as to win those under the law. To those not having the law I became like one not having the law...so as to win those not having the law. To the weak I became weak, to win the weak. I have become all things to all men so that by all possible means I might save some. **I do all this for the sake of the gospel*** (1 Corinthians 9:20-23).

When Peter came to Antioch, I opposed him to his face, because he was clearly in the wrong. Before certain men came from James, he used to eat with the Gentiles. But when they arrived, he began to draw back and separate himself from the Gentiles because he was afraid of those who belonged to the circumcision group. The other Jews joined him in his hypocrisy, so that by their hypocrisy even Barnabas was led astray (Galatians 2:11-13).

*And when you pray, do not be like the hypocrites, for they love to pray
standing in the synagogues and on the street corners to be seen by
men...But when you pray, go into your room, close the door and pray
to your Father, who is unseen...And when you pray, do not keep on
babbling like pagans, for they think they will be heard because of their
many words. Do not be like them, for your Father knows what you
need before you ask him* (Matthew 6:5-8).

*Woe to you, teachers of the law and Pharisees, you hypocrites! You
give a tenth of your spices—mint, dill and cummin. But you have
neglected the more important matters of the law—justice, mercy and
faithfulness. You should have practiced the latter, without neglecting
the former. You blind guides! You strain out a gnat but swallow a
camel* (Matthew 23:23-24).

So long as you are true to the commandments of God about moral and
spiritual issues, you need not be overly concerned about anything else. You
do not need to know the dimensions of the Jewish tabernacle. You do not
need to know how old Methuselah was or who his granddaddy was. You do
not need to know when or how God created the world. Such things are
issues for scientists, historians and theologians to sort out.

But what you do need to know, what is essential that you know, are the
commandments of God. Therefore, "as members one of another," we should
all continue our search, honestly and objectively, with charity in our hearts,
for a fuller understanding of the Scriptures that affect our salvation. Even
then we will "live by faith, not by sight" (2 Corinthians 5:7). The cause of
Christ would be better served if we kept this in mind and remembered that
unyielding and dogmatic declarations about non-spiritual issues can be
offensive to many Christians:

*It has long troubled me that religious authorities try to cram God's
beautiful and wonderful creation into six 24-hour days. My job, for
almost ten years, was to make mechanical, electrical and radioactive
records of the earth's formations to depths in excess of three miles.
These formations were laid down in sequence and can be traced and
correlated from Canada to Mexico and from West Virginia to*

Wyoming and beyond. Some are coal beds formed from decaying veg-etation. Some are sandstone, shale or gravel laid down as sediments. Other formations are limestone laid down in seas or oceans as evi-denced by fossils of fish and seashells. Still other formations contain igneous rocks formed from volcanoes or from molten materiel that came from deep within the earth's core. I believe that God has pro-vided us with an orderly sequence of events that demonstrate creation took place over millions of years (Charles Wilderson, retired petroleum engineer).

Many of Charles' brothers and sisters in Christ do not agree with him. They believe that creation took place within a six-day period of time. Yet they hold him in the highest esteem. Why? Because he is a model of one in whom Christ lives, filled with fruits of the Spirit (Galatians 2:20; 5:22-26). And, in the spirit of Christian charity, he, likewise, does not diminish his respect and appreciation for these good friends. But in this letter to the author he lets us know how uncharitable some "religious authorities" have been on this issue and how it makes him feel. Yet, because he is a strong and devoted Christian, Charles ignores them and goes on about his Master's business.

But it should make all of us wonder how many spiritually weaker souls have been lost over this **and a host of other matters** that have little to do with the message of the cross of Jesus Christ. Especially vulnerable are our young men and women in secular institutions of learning. All due to the fact that both theologians and less qualified teachers have too often forgot-ten that **the Bible, first, foremost, and last, is a spiritual book—Gods' message of salvation to a lost and dying world!** And that the length of the days of creation **or any other opinion about non-spiritual matters** will not be listed as part of the standards by which we stand or fall when God judges the thoughts and intents of the heart:

But the things that come out of the mouth come from the heart, and these make a man "unclean." For out of the heart come evil thoughts, murder, adultery, sexual immorality, theft, false testimony, slander. These are what make a man "unclean"; but eating with unwashed hands does not make him "unclean" (Matthew 15:18-20).

Let us stop passing judgment on one another. Instead, make up your mind not to put any stumbling block or obstacle in your brother's way...Let us...make every effort to do what leads to peace and to mutual edification (Romans 14:13-19).

The goal of this command is love, which comes from a pure heart and a good conscience and a sincere faith (1 Timothy 1:4-6).

Blessed are the pure in heart, for they will see God (Matthew 5:8).

What I have written in this chapter is not intended to discourage anyone from pursuing a deeper study of God's word as it relates to obscure prophecies and relationships to scientific and historical issues. In fact, there are many good books, written by both Christians and non-Christians, that can help in pursuing such studies. But this is not the place to start. I well remember the words of my old and beloved mentor when, shortly after I became a Christian, I asked him to help me study the book of Revelation. He said, "Calvin, after you have diligently studied the Bible for about fifteen years, you will still be about ten years shy of being ready. That is, if you have also become very knowledgeable about world history and ancient cultures."

No doubt he was exaggerating the requirements, but A. R. Kepple, an outstanding Gospel preacher, was simply telling me that **both our understanding of the Scriptures and application of their teachings is a process of growth!** He was not discouraging me from reading the book of Revelation or any other part of the Bible that is filled with difficult things to understand. But the in-depth study I was seeking would ignore the fact that a new Christian is considered to be a "babe" in Christ that "grows" to spiritual maturity by concentrating on the spiritual focus of God's word— "the grace and knowledge of our Lord and Savior Jesus Christ!" (2 Peter 3:18) Even this does not happen overnight:

I have much more to say to you, more than you can now bear (John 16:12)...*Therefore, rid yourselves of all malice and all deceit, hypocrisy, envy, and slander of every kind. Like newborn babies, crave pure spiritual milk, so that by it you may grow up in your salvation* (1 Peter 2:1-2)...*But solid food is for the mature, who by constant use have trained themselves to distinguish good from evil* (Hebrews 5:14).

For this very reason, make every effort to add to your faith goodness; and to goodness, knowledge; and to knowledge, self-control; and to self-control, perseverance; and to perseverance, godliness; and to godliness, brotherly kindness; and to brotherly kindness, love. For if you possess these qualities in increasing measure, they will keep you from being ineffective and unproductive in your knowledge of our Lord Jesus Christ (2 Peter 1:5-8).

But wherever we are in our honest and sincere quest for knowledge, even if only "newborn babies" in Christ, **we are accepted by Him** as much as those who have labored all their lives and understand a great deal about the Bible. For when all is said and done, **we are all unworthy:**

For the kingdom of heaven is like a landowner who went out early in the morning to hire men to work in his vineyard. He agreed to pay them a denarius for the day and sent them into his vineyard. About the third hour he went out and saw others standing in the marketplace doing nothing. He told them, "You also go and work in my vineyard, and I will pay you whatever is right." So they went. He went out again about the sixth hour and the ninth hour and did the same thing. About the eleventh hour he went out and found still others standing around. He asked them, "Why have you been standing here all day long doing nothing?" "Because no one has hired us," they answered. He said to them, "You also go and work in my vineyard." When evening came, the owner of the vineyard said to his foreman, "Call the workers and pay them their wages, beginning with the last ones hired and going on to the first." The workers who were hired about the eleventh hour came and each received a denarius. So when those came who were hired first, they expected to receive more. But each one of them also received a denarius. When they received it, they began to grumble against the

landowner. "These men who were hired last worked only one hour,"
they said, "and you have made them equal to us who have borne the
burden of the work and the heat of the day." But he answered one
of them, "Friend, I am not being unfair to you. Didn't you agree to
work for a denarius? Take your pay and go. I want to give the man
who was hired last the same as I gave you. Don't I have the right
to do what I want with my own money? Or are you envious because
I am generous?" So the last will be first, and the first will be last
(Matthew 20:1-16).

So you also, when you have done everything you were told to do,
should say, "We are unworthy servants; we have only done our duty"
(Luke 17:10).

There is no difference, *for all have sinned and fall short of the glory*
of God, and are justified freely by his grace through the redemption
that came by Christ Jesus (Romans 3:22-24).

Having laid the groundwork for spiritual growth, I must now turn my
attention to two things that have perplexed so many young men and
women—the Genesis account of creation and the theory of evolution.
Traditional approaches by theologians have failed to provide sufficient
information to effectively answer the questions of millions of young and
inquiring minds. Simply saying, "The Bible says so, so it must be true," is
not enough. There must be a reasonable **correlation** of what they hear on
Sunday with what they can observe in the laboratory on Monday.
Otherwise, the loss of our young people will only get worse. I have devoted
six years of my life to find that correlation and stem the tide. Some of these
explanations may at first be hard to grasp but it is a difficulty that cannot
be avoided.

Without doubt, the two most difficult things to overcome were my
own paradigms of thought and the influence of religious writers and speak-
ers—"The mind is slow in unlearning what it has been long in learning"
(Seneca). To say that we will go to enormous lengths to prove and tenaciously hold on to our "positions" is an understatement, even when faced

with legitimate evidence to the contrary. No better examples can be found than the rejection and crucifixion of Jesus Himself and the hundreds of different and competing denominations, each claiming "their way" is the Bible way. I pray that my work on this book will be a start in tearing down those walls of division.

Who is this that darkens my counsel with words without knowledge? Brace yourself like a man; I will question you, and you shall answer me.

Where were you when I laid the earth's foundation? Tell me, if you understand. Who marked off its dimensions? Surely you know! Who stretched a measuring line across it? On what were its footings set, or who laid its cornerstone—while the morning stars sang together and all the angels shouted for joy?

Job 38:2-7

CHAPTER THREE

The Genesis Account of Creation

ANYONE WHO BELIEVES WHAT GOD TOLD JOB SHOULD KNOW THAT delving into creation is like finding and analyzing a black hole in space—more mystery than knowledge—**no human being was there!** God has given us less information about creation than almost any other subject in the Bible. In fact, there are only a few more words devoted to creation than what He told the Israelites about the clothing they could and could not wear or the adulterous relationship between David and Bathsheba, and only a fraction of the instructions provided for construction of the Jewish tabernacle and articles of worship.

So, let me begin this chapter with a confession: **I do not know** how or when God created the heavens and the earth. **Neither do I know** when or how He created "all" of the various "kinds" of vegetation and animals. **Nor do I know** when He created Adam and Eve or when He brought the great flood upon the earth. **But I believe that He did!** Beyond recognition of the presence and involvement of God in all these things, the most that I can do is cherish my own "opinion" and in turn respect the opinions of

71

others—**unless those opinions diminish the Gospel of Christ or challenge the existence and power of the Almighty God!**

Having said this, let me present some of the reasons why I believe it is impossible to develop an authoritative religious or scientific doctrine, in any great detail, on the subject of creation. Impossible from the Scriptures because of the **extremely limited amount of information** God has chosen to reveal. And impossible from scientific investigations because of the **inherent limitations imposed by the laws of nature.** Including the fact that nature, to an unknown degree, began in a state of **apparent age!**

Of course, it is easy to read the first chapter of Genesis, along with Exodus 20:11, and conclude that God created everything in six, twenty-four-hour days. It is also fairly easy to count the generations that are listed in the Bible and determine that creation took place about six thousand years ago. Moreover, there are a few scientists who believe this conclusion has some merit in physical evidence. But since this belief is so well documented in religious teachings, both oral and written, I shall only briefly mention the scientific evidence supporting these conclusions after presenting another view of the creative process. A view that I pray will not offend or diminish the beauty of a belief system that, for a long period of time, has given comfort of mind and strength of purpose to millions of people in both living and sharing the Gospel of Christ.

However, as mentioned in the previous chapter, there are many Christians, especially in the scientific community, who believe that creation took place many thousands, millions or even billions of years ago. It is for these brothers and sisters-in-Christ, and for those outside the church who are struggling with the validity of the Bible itself, that this chapter is written. My objective is to show that this belief is not totally dependent on scientific research but also on considerable evidence within the Bible itself. Consider, for example, the Sabbath day, the "seventh day" of creation:

> *By the seventh day God had finished the work he had been doing; so on the seventh day he rested from all his work. And God blessed the seventh day and made it holy, because on it he rested from all the work of creating that he had done* (Genesis 2:2-3).

For in six days the LORD made the heavens and the earth, the sea, and all that is in them, but he rested on the seventh day. Therefore the LORD blessed the Sabbath day and made it holy (Exodus 20:11).

This seems clear enough except that making the seventh day a literal, twenty-four hour period of rest is inconsistent with the very nature of God:

Do you not know? Have you not heard? The LORD is the everlasting God, the Creator of the ends of the earth. He will not grow tired or weary, and his understanding no one can fathom. He gives strength to the weary and increases the power of the weak (Isaiah 40:28-29).

Isaiah's God did "not grow tired or weary," like we do, rest for twenty-four hours, and then go back to the work of running the universe on the eighth day. Consistent with this fact is that the writer of Hebrews identifies the seventh day as continuous and unending:

Now we who have believed enter that rest, just as God has said, "So I declared on oath in my anger, 'They shall never enter my rest.'" And yet his work has been finished since the creation of the world. For somewhere he has spoken about the seventh day in these words: "And on the seventh day God rested from all his work." And again in the passage above he says, "They shall never enter my rest." It still remains that some will enter that rest ... there **remains** *then a Sabbath rest...***for anyone who enters God's rest also rests from his own work, just as God did from his.** *Let us, therefore, make every effort to enter that rest* (Hebrews 4:3-11).

God entered a "rest" on the "seventh day" that still **"remains."** The writer of Hebrews uses the "seventh day" as a **metaphor for an indeterminate period of time!** Why, then, would we consider the previous six "days" as anything other than metaphors as well? Especially when we know that the same Hebrew word for "day" is used for all seven days. So far as time is concerned, the only difference is that each of the first six days had both a beginning and ending. Isn't it reasonable to conclude that the seventh day provides us with a **contextual model** for the preceding six days—a model showing that the previous six days were not limited to a period of twenty-four hours. On what basis would we arrive at any other conclusion?

But how does this interpretation correlate with the requirement to observe the Sabbath, the seventh day of each week? It's true that God justified the Sabbath observance by the Jews by referring to the creative week. But does this mean God intended it to always be used in this sense? Apparently not, for we know that the Sabbath day of rest was never mentioned as either a religious or secular observance prior to the time it was given to the Jewish people in Exodus 16:23. **It is a command peculiar to the Law of Moses!** There is no indication that Adam or even Abraham observed it. Nor Christians, whose day of rest is "everlasting." If the purpose of the Sabbath was always deemed to be a holy day because of creation, a universal issue for all mankind, **why this omission for people other than the Jews?** Perhaps this is why Jesus identified the Sabbath observance by the Jews as something that was "made for man" [as a] "day of rest" (Exodus 31:14-17; Mark 2:23-28).

It appears most likely that God, in the Mosaical law, **presented a word picture of six creative days**, followed with a "day of rest," as a means of helping the Jewish people understand, as a nation of people, the importance of "rest" for both physical and emotional well-being, and as a marker around which so many aspects of their worship and civil laws were built. While it may be argued that, from a human perspective, a weekly day of rest would be good for anyone, the Sabbath "day," by God's own choice, is noticeably absent from the Christian law. Instead, the exact same Scripture (Genesis 2:2-3), used as a literal day in the Jewish law, is now used as the basis for an "everlasting" day of rest for those who accept Christ as their Savior (John 6:47; Hebrews 4:3-11). As a day of worship, **it is specifically excluded:**

> *Therefore do not let anyone judge you by what you eat or drink, or with regard to a religious festival, a New Moon celebration or a Sabbath day. These are a shadow of the things that were to come; the reality, however, is found in Christ* (Colossians 2:16-17).

This text reminds us that whether it was the Jewish "Sabbath," a "religious festival," or the "sanctuary" and other "copies" of heavenly things (Hebrews 8:5; 9:23), their purpose was to be "only a shadow of the good things that are coming—not the realities themselves." (Hebrews 10:1). The **reality** is that the seventh day following creation was an **eternal** "rest" into which God entered—not a twenty-four hour period of time (Hebrews 4:1-11). Only later, as a part of Jewish law, did God construct the account of creation to give it the appearance of a literal day. A day that, like the rest of the law, ended when it was "nailed to the cross" Colossians 2:13-14; Galatians 3:19-25). It was in the replacement law, the law of Christ, that God revealed the real, eternal nature of the seventh day.

Another consideration is that "numbers with symbolic significance fig- ure prominently in Genesis...the number seven...quite frequently" (NIV Bible, Introduction to Genesis). To discount at least the possibility of this type of **symbolism** in constructing a creative week of indeterminate length in the first chapter of Genesis seems to be unwarranted. Especially when every theologian knows that such linguistic idioms occur throughout the entire Bible, often compressing very long periods of time into a "day" or "week." And that the number seven is especially used to indicate complete- ness rather than literal time.

The difficulty in determining the length of each creative day and even the **sequence** of "all" events are further compounded by what is revealed in the following Scriptures—Scriptures that give a clear indication of events that occurred **earlier** than when first mentioned or **overlapped** from one day to the next. Key words that will be discussed are **highlighted**:

> **Genesis 1:1-31:**
> **Day one:** *In the beginning God created the **heavens** and the earth...the Spirit of God was hovering over the waters. And God said, "Let there be **light**"...God called the light "**day**," and the **dark- ness** he called "**night**."*
>
> **Day two:** *God said, "Let there be an expanse between the waters to separate water from water." So God made the expanse and **separated the water under the expanse from the water above it.***
>
> **Day three:** *God said, "Let the water under the sky be gathered to one place, and let **dry ground** appear." God called the dry ground "land," and the gathered waters he called "seas."...Then God said, "Let the*

land produce vegetation: **seed-bearing plants and trees on the land that bear fruit with seed in it,** according to their various kinds."

Day four: God said, "Let there be **lights** in the expanse of the sky to **separate the day from the night,** and let them serve as signs to mark seasons and days and years, and let them be lights in the expanse of the sky to give light **on the earth.**"...God made two great lights—the greater light to govern the day and the lesser light to govern the night. He also made the stars. God set them in the expanse of the sky to give light on the earth, to govern the day and the night, and to **separate light from darkness.**

Day five: God said, "Let the water teem with living creatures, and let birds fly above the earth across the expanse of the sky." So God created the great creatures of the sea and every living and moving thing with which the water teems, according to their kinds, and every winged bird according to its kind.

Day six: God said, "Let the land produce living creatures according to their kinds: livestock, creatures that move along the ground, and wild animals, each according to its kind."...Then God said, "Let us make man in our image, in our likeness, and let them rule over the fish of the sea and the birds of the air, over the livestock, over all the earth, and over all the creatures that move along the ground." So God created man in his own image, in the image of God he created him; male and female he created them...God saw all that he had made, and it was very good.

Genesis 2:1-7:

1. Thus the heavens and the earth were completed in all their vast array.

2. By the seventh day God had finished the work he had been doing; so on the seventh day he rested from all his work.

3. And God blessed the seventh day and made it holy, because on it he rested from all the work of creating that he had done.

4. This is the account of the **heavens** and the earth when they were **created.** When the LORD God made the earth and the heavens—

5. *and no shrub of the field had yet appeared on the earth and no plant of the field had yet sprung up,* **FOR** *the* LORD *God had not sent rain* **on the earth** *and there was no man to work the ground,*

6. **but streams came up from the earth and watered the whole surface of the ground—**

7. *The* LORD *God formed the man from the dust of the ground and breathed into his nostrils the breath of life, and the man became a living being.*

8. *Now the* LORD *God had planted a garden in the east, in Eden; and there he put the man he had formed.*

9. *And the* LORD *God made all kinds of trees grow out of the ground— trees that were pleasing to the eye and good for food. In the middle of the garden were the tree of life and the tree of the knowledge of good and evil.*

10. **A river watering the garden** *flowed from Eden; from there it was separated into four headwaters.*

Hebrews 11:3: *The universe was formed at God's command, so that what is seen was not made out of what was visible.*

Isaiah 45:12: *My own hands stretched out the* **heavens;** *I marshaled their* **starry** *hosts.*

Jeremiah 8:2: *They will be exposed to the* **sun** *and the* **moon** *and all the* **stars** *of the* **heavens.**

Psalm 8:3: *I consider your* **heavens,** *the work of your fingers,* **the moon and the stars,** *which you have* **set in place.**

Proverbs 8:27-29: *When he* **set the heavens in place,** *when he* **marked out the horizon on the face of the deep,** *when he* **established the clouds above** *and fixed securely the fountains of the deep, when he* **gave the sea its boundary** *so the waters would not overstep his command, and when he* **marked out the foundations of the earth.**

Job 38:4-7: *Where were you when I laid the earth's foundation? Tell me, if you understand. Who marked off its dimensions? Surely you know! Who stretched a measuring line across it? On what were its footings set, or who laid its cornerstone—**while the morning stars sang together** and all the angels shouted for joy?*

Job 38:8-11: *Who shut up the sea behind doors when it burst forth from the womb, when **I made the clouds its garment and wrapped it in thick darkness**, when I fixed limits for it and set its doors and bars in place, when I said, "This far you may come and no farther; here is where your proud waves halt"?*

By placing each of these Scriptural commentaries beside the related event in the first chapter of Genesis, a picture emerges of a creative process that began at God's command and then went through a largely natural series of events whereby the planet became hospitable to both plant and animal life. A natural process that in and of itself is as much an act of God as the initial creation. God is not just the author of matter but also the natural laws that govern its behavior—laws so definite and predictable that we can use them to split an atom, send men to the moon, or even clone a living plant or animal. The most complete parallel accounts of the creative week are found in the books of Genesis and Proverbs:

Genesis 1:1-10	Proverbs 8:27-29
God created the heavens… and light…and separated day and night	He set the heavens in place
Darkness was over the surface of the deep	When he marked out the horizon on the face of the deep
Let there be an expanse between the waters to separate water from water	When he established the clouds above and fixed securely the fountains of the deep
Let the water under the sky be gathered to one place, and let the dry ground appear	He gave the sea its boundary

He marked out the foundations of the earth |

These parallel accounts cover the first two and one-half days of the creation week. From these two accounts, it seems that the "heavens" were not only created on the first day but also "set…in place." It also appears from the following Scriptures that the "heavens" of the first day were what we see today—the sun, moon and stars:

Isaiah 45:12: My own hands stretched out the **heavens***; I marshaled their* **starry** *hosts*

Psalm 8:3: I consider your **heavens***…the* **moon and stars***, which you have* **set in place**

Jeremiah 8:2: They will be exposed to the **sun** *and the* **moon** *and all the* **stars** *of the* **heavens**

Deuteronomy 4:19: And when you look up to the sky and see the **sun***, the* **moon** *and the* **stars***—all* **the heavenly array***—*

Job 38:4-7: Where were you when I laid the earth's foundation?…while the **morning stars** *sang together*

Even in Job's poetic description, the "morning stars" were present when God laid the earth's foundation, an event that happened **prior to the fourth day** of the creative week when, as generally supposed, the stars were first created. It is also worth noting that the same Hebrew word for "heavens," used in the Genesis account of creation, was also used in the other referenced Scriptures—Scriptures that clearly identify the "heavens" of Genesis 1:1 as the sun, moon and stars.

Establishment of the sun, moon and stars would also be consistent with the creation of "light" on the first day. If these are not the heavenly bodies from which light emanated on the first day, what was? And what was it that God used to separate "day" and "night" and "evening and "morning" except the orbital relationship between the sun and the earth? **There is not the slightest hint in the entire Bible of any other substance or source of light than the sun, moon and stars!** Moreover, Genesis 2:4-5 specifically states that these physical "heavens" **preceded** the appearance of "vegetation," an event that took place on the third day. This apparent contradiction between the events described for the first and fourth days will be discussed a little later. But now part of the parallel account in Proverbs is repeated, for your convenience, to illustrate additional details about the first part of the creative week:

Let there be an expanse between the waters to separate water from water	When he established the clouds above and fixed securely the fountains of the deep
Let the water under the sky be gathered to one place, and let the dry ground appear	He gave the sea its boundary He marked out the foundations of the earth

As before, the parallel account in Proverbs adds detail that is **omitted** in the Genesis account, identifying the waters above the expanse as "clouds." It is also clear that the "fountains of the deep" refer to a liquid planet. For it was from a liquid "sea" that God made the "dry ground" appear. The events of the second and third days are further clarified by an analysis of the following Scriptures:

Psalm 24:1-2: *The earth is the LORD's, and everything in it, the world, and all who live in it; for he founded it upon the seas and established it upon the waters.*

Job 38:4-11: *Where were you when I laid the earth's foundation?...while the morning stars sang together...Who shut up the sea behind doors when it burst forth from the womb, when I made the clouds its garment and wrapped it in thick darkness.*

Genesis 2:4-6: *This is the account of the heavens and the earth when they were created. When the Lord God made the earth and the heavens—and no shrub of the field had yet appeared on the earth and no plant of the field had yet sprung up, FOR the Lord God had not sent rain on the earth and there was no man to work the ground, but streams [mists]*[13] *came up and watered the whole surface of the ground.*

---

13. Translated "mists" in most versions of the Bible.

Genesis 2:10: A **river watering the garden** *flowed from Eden; from there it was separated into four headwaters.*

These Scriptures picture an earth "wrapped" in clouds so dense as to leave it in a state of "thick darkness" and "upward mists [that]...watered the whole surface of the ground," **prior** to the time it became "dry." These Scriptures also tell us that it was **after** the mists ceased, but **before** the appearance of vegetation, it began to **"rain on the earth."** Additional credence to this interpretation is found in the meaning of the Hebrew word **"for"** in Genesis 2:5: "a primitive particle [the full form of the prepositional prefix] indicating **causal** relations."[14] Another element is the parenthetical remark, "there was no man to work the ground," clearly indicating that the normal patterns of nature were essential precursors to man's ability to "work the ground."

In short, the **reason** there was no vegetation prior to the third day is because it had not yet rained "on the earth," **an essential precursor** "for" that creative event. This is not scientific theory. **This is a Biblical description** of what appears to have been a long and natural process whereby a hot and liquid planet, with attendant "mists," eventually cooled enough to allow development of normal weather patterns—weather patterns sufficient to sustain vegetation on "dry" ground (Genesis 1:9-13).

To give further weight to the interpretation that the days of Genesis were longer than a few hours and that the mists gradually gave way to normal patterns of rain is the fact that Genesis 2:10 reveals there was a "river watering" the Garden of Eden, where Adam lived. A river so large it fed four additional rivers. If the river's source were from the upward "mists" that **"watered the whole surface of the ground,"** why would Adam have needed a "river" to water what was already wet? And why would God have even mentioned the "mists" if they lasted only a few hours? But if, by the time Adam was created, the forces of modern nature were at work, including the intermittent nature of rain, there is no inconsistency between the "mists" of Genesis 2:6 and the "river" of Genesis 2:10.

---

14. *Biblesoft's New Exhaustive Strong's Numbers and Concordance with Expanded Greek-Hebrew Dictionary.* Copyright (c) 1994, Biblesoft and International Bible Translators, Inc.

Can you imagine the Garden of Eden as a place where the ground was so wet and muddy that it provided enough water to feed these rivers? Or a place where the sun did not shine because it was blanketed by a "thick darkness [of] clouds"? Doesn't it seem more likely that both of these dreary conditions were gone by the fourth day when the sun was clearly visible "on the earth"? And certainly by the sixth day when Adam was created? What possible reason would God have for revealing these conditions of nature except to let us have a peek into creative processes that lasted much longer than a few hours?

Perhaps, over the centuries, one of the most perplexing problems for theologians has been the event described for the fourth day. According to the first chapter of Genesis, the sun, moon and stars were "made" on the fourth day. Yet, as already discussed, the Bible clearly indicates they were not only "created" but also "set in place" **on the first day!** Why, then, does the Bible tell us they were "made" on the fourth day?

First, we need to understand that the Hebrew word used for "created" on the first day is not used in the account of the fourth day's activities. A different word is used and is translated as "made." While this may or may not be of significance, it is significant that the Bible, when denoting the distinction between day and night, uses the same Hebrew words and terminology on the fourth day as that of the first:

> **Genesis 1:3-5:** *And God said, "Let there be light," and there was light. God saw that the light was good, and he **separated the light from the darkness.** God called the light "**day**," and the darkness he called "**night**." And there was **evening**, and there was **morning**—the first day.*

> **Genesis 1:14-19:** *And God said, "Let there be lights in the expanse of the sky to **separate** the **day** from the **night**…to **separate light from darkness.** And there was **evening**, and there was **morning**—the fourth day.*

If the same terminology is used, along with the Scriptural indication that the "heavens" were "set in place" on the first day, it seems that whatever is said about the fourth day must be something other than the actual creation and orbital placement of the sun, moon and stars. Perhaps our failure to recognize this fact throughout the years is no different than the mistake experienced by Martin Luther regarding the orbit of the earth:

> *People gave ear to an upstart astrologer who strove to show that the Earth revolves, not the heavens or the firmament, the sun and moon... This fool Copernicus wishes to reverse the entire science of astronomy; but sacred Scripture tells us that Joshua commanded the sun to stand still and not the earth.*

Luther was wrong! He simply failed to understand that, from an earthly perspective, the sun **appeared** to stand still. In the same way, from an earthly perspective, the sun **appeared** to have been made on the fourth day. The fact that no one was around to view it does not change the possibility that God was presenting the account from an earthly perspective, as He did with Joshua. And why would God have created vegetation before creating the sun, an essential source of heat and light?

It appears that God may have simply provided us with a word picture, a **literary arrangement**, showing the sun, moon and stars as they eventually appeared to and were used, by the Israelites and all other people, for light and timekeepers "on the earth." Such an interpretation seems to be consistent with what we previously learned about rain "on the earth"—a weather event that did not occur until some time **after** the clouds and the mists had dissipated through the natural cooling of the earth. Not that the clouds did not produce rain, but in its infancy the earth would have probably been so hot it would have vaporized the rain before it reached the surface of the planet. Only after it had sufficiently cooled would the "upward mists" have gradually given way to rain "on the earth." Why, then, would it seem unnatural for Moses to have used the same terminology to describe a previously existing sun that had not as yet fully shined "on the earth" without cloud interference?

Scientists have speculated that the atmosphere was created by widespread volcanic eruptions from an earth that was initially very hot and unstable. This, of course, is pure speculation—they were not there. However, the idea of a hot planet is certainly consistent with the possibilities just discussed. Especially when we know that the interior of our planet is, even today, in a hot, liquid state. In fact, temperatures just five miles below the surface may be as high as 1,600 degrees, hot enough to melt rocks, and the center of the earth as much as 9,000 degrees.

This would also be a good time to address the belief by many people that it did not rain prior to the Great Flood—a belief resting on the fact that the rainbow is not mentioned until after this catastrophic event (Genesis 9:12-16). It was at this time that God chose it as a sign or seal of His covenant with man to never again destroy the earth with such a flood. Yet, as earlier noted, Genesis 2:5 specifically stated that it began to rain **prior** to the appearance of vegetation and man. This, coupled with the fact that the sun was also made visible "on the earth" (Genesis 1:17), **prior** to the creation of man, means that the essential elements for a rainbow also existed **prior** to the flood. Even before it rained "on the earth" the sun, shining through the "streams" or "mists" of water, would have produced rainbows. This is but another example where, by use of relevant Scriptures, we can identify that an event actually took place **earlier** than when it is first mentioned in the Bible:

> The seal of this covenant of nature was natural enough; it was the rainbow, which, it is likely, was seen in the clouds before, when second causes concurred, but was never a seal of the covenant till now that it was made so by a divine institution (Matthew Henry's Commentary).

> From the well-known cause of this phenomenon it cannot be rationally supposed that there was no rainbow in the heavens before the time mentioned in the text, for as the rainbow is the natural effect of the sun's rays falling on drops of water, and of their being refracted and reflected by them, it must have appeared at different times from the creation of the sun and the atmosphere. Nor does the text intimate that the bow was now created for a sign to Noah and his posterity; but that what was formerly created, or rather that which was the necessary effect, in certain cases, of the creation of the sun and atmosphere, should now be considered by them as an unfailing token of their continual preservation from the waters of a deluge; therefore the text

speaks of what had already been done, and not of what was now done
(*Adam Clark Commentary*).

To further deepen the mystery of creative time, it appears that whatever took place on the sixth day took a lot longer than a few hours:

> *Now the LORD God had formed out of the ground all the beasts of the field and all the birds of the air. He brought them to the man to see what he would name them; and whatever the man called each living creature, that was its name. So the man gave names to all the livestock, the birds of the air and all the beasts of the field. But for Adam no suitable helper was found... Then the LORD God made a woman from the rib he had taken out of the man* (Genesis 2:19-22).

If the traditional interpretation of a twenty-four hour day is correct, and everything mentioned is to be taken in a completely literal sense, it poses some inspiring logistical problems. How could one man examine "all" livestock and "all" birds and "all" beasts in order to assign an appropriate name as well as take the time to determine if a "suitable helper" could be found? Even if Adam only dealt with the original "kinds," it would still be an exceptionally large number of animals that would have to be processed at an extremely fast pace—even faster if done only in the daylight hours. That may have been why the Revised Standard Version states, when referring to the final act of the sixth day, "This **at last** is bone of my bones and flesh of my flesh; she shall be called Woman" (Genesis 2:23).

Moreover, the word "all" poses another problem for a literal application of all words and phrases. Aside from the daunting task of inspecting all land and air animals, of what benefit would there be to Adam in giving a distinct name to something he would never see again and that lived thousands of miles from Eden? Perhaps a more reasonable assessment is that the word is nothing more than a commonly used hyperbolic expression that referred only to those animals with which Adam and his family would have contact in the Garden of Eden.

Such limitations contained in the words "all,""everyone," and other similar expressions occur quite frequently in the Scriptures. For example, 1 Samuel (chapter 15) declares that the Amalekites were "totally destroyed...men, women and children." Yet shortly thereafter (chapter 28) the Israelites were at war with them again. In this case, the all-encompassing hyperbolic expression obviously referred only to those Amalekites the Israelites encountered in this one battle.

Moses himself, author of the books of Genesis through Deuteronomy, used a similar hyperbolic expression when admonishing the Israelites to follow God's laws and be blessed. "Then **all** the peoples on earth will see that you are called by the name of the LORD, and they will fear you" (Deuteronomy 28:10-11). It is apparent that "all" was limited to those who were close enough to be acquainted with the nation of Israel. On what basis would we rule out the possibility that such usage of the word also applied to the encounter Adam had with the animals in Eden? The same man was the author of both statements.

In summary, from nothing came something—**God created!** The earth He created was a dark, liquid planet, "formless and empty, darkness was over the surface of the deep, and the Spirit of God was hovering over the waters" (Genesis 1:2). And then God said, "let there be light" (Genesis 1:3). Light is not a new substance but a mode or condition of heated matter. Science cannot tell us why this occurs. It can only observe that it does:

> *[Let there be light], [Y_hiy (OT:1961) 'owr (OT:216)]. It is deserv-*
> *ing of particular notice that the substantive verb is used here, and not*
> *either [baaraa' (OT:1254)] 'created' or ['aasaah (OT:6213)]*
> *'made.' It was manifestation of what had been previously in exis-*
> *tence-'Let light be,' or rather, 'Light shall be;' not the formation of an*
> *element or matter which had no being at all until this divine com-*
> *mand was issued. The effect, which immediately followed, is described*
> *in the name DAY, which in Hebrew signifies warmth, heat; while the*
> *name NIGHT signifies a rolling up, as night wraps all things in a*
> *shady mantle* (Jamieson, Fausset, and Brown Commentary, Electronic
> Database. Copyright © 1997 by Biblesoft).

Subsequent to initial creation, apparently through natural processes, the earth produced "upward mists" and a blanket of "clouds" so "thick" that it was "wrapped" in "darkness." Simply heating a kettle of water and watching the rising steam is a minuscule example of what it may have been like. As the hot planet cooled, the mists and thickness of the clouds gradually dissipated, allowing normal weather patterns of both rain and sunshine "on the earth." Thus, the planet is made ready for life. Such an interpretation considers the days of Genesis to be metaphors for a process that would have taken far longer than a few days.

None of this is to say that God could not create the earth and its inhabitants in six literal days. He, of course, could have done anything He chose to do. But we cannot legitimately dismiss the implications of what the Scriptures tell us about the creative process in places other than the first chapter of Genesis—Scriptures that clearly seem to indicate it occurred over a much longer period of time.

Neither can we dismiss the testimony of nature that offers an abundance of data that creation took place a long time ago, such as the existence of uncountable galaxies of stars and planets where distance can only be measured in light years and where we find evidence of explosions, movement, dead stars, comets, meteorites and black holes—things that cannot be seen with the naked eye, much less visit, and that serve no apparent human need.

Another compelling bit of physical evidence for believing in an earth that is much older than a few thousand years is found in the mind-boggling quantity of fossil fuels that would, under normal circumstances, require millions of years to form.[15] Another thing difficult to dismiss is that scientists have extracted ice cores from glaciers and, like reading the rings on a tree stump, have been able to physically count the passing of seasons, revealing an earth that appears to have been around for over 200,000 years. As D. E. Wonderly said:

We are by no means in a position of having to struggle to find evidence for great age in the earth. There is a veritable avalanche of

---

15. The most pessimistic authorities would agree that there is at least five million million tons, if you include seams too narrow to be worth mining. This works out at sixty-five pounds of coal for every square yard of our planet's land surface. Where did the vegetation come from to produce all that coal?...It takes a lot of wood to produce a little coal...Coal...is mostly composed of the remains of large fern like plants." (Alan Hayward, *Creation and Evolution:* Bethany House Publishers, Minneapolis, Minnesota, pages 126-127).

such evidence (D. E. Wonderly, *God's Time-Records in Ancient Sediments*, Crystal Press, Michigan, page 65).

While many details withheld from the ancient Israelites are becoming understood by advancements in knowledge, the Bible, both then and now, is a relevant revelation of creation by a supernatural being. No other similar religious document provides such a rational and logical correlation with the natural world:

> *If I as a geologist were called upon to explain briefly our modern ideas of the origin of the earth and the development of life on it to a simple, pastoral people, such as the tribes to whom the Book of Genesis was addressed, I could hardly do better than follow rather closely much of the language of the first chapter of Genesis* (The Lamp, "The Worlds of Wallace Pratt," by W. L. Copithorne, Fall 1971, page 14).

> *God gave his word as a religious guide and not as a history or science book. He spoke to a primitive people in a language they could comprehend about their world. Words used were to convey meaning to them in their culture and time. Otherwise why didn't he tell them about the laws of gravity, relativity, atoms and other natural laws by which his universe is governed? To try to fit modern scientific and historical knowledge into the words left as a religious guide takes away the faith of our walk and makes our walk by sight…God gave limited information to a knowledge limited people* (Bob Ritter, in a letter to the author).

The latter statement is from a Bible and history teacher. The first statement is from a highly respected geologist. Both of these men, though with vastly different education and experience backgrounds, seem to have come to the same basic conclusion—the Bible, while providing some insight into the creative process, is a spiritual book that was never intended to be a comprehensive textbook on the **details** of physical science. The comment by Bob Ritter, "God gave limited information to a knowledge limited people," is similar to the statement made by Jesus, "I have much more to say to you, more than you can now bear" (John 16:12).

Now comes the most perplexing problem—life! As previously noted, on day two and the first part of day three, God used previously created matter to fashion and form the atmosphere and dry land. But during the latter part of day three, God performed the amazing and miraculous act of giving life to inert material. From the "ground" came living vegetation with the inherent capability of reproduction "according to their various kinds." On days five and six animal life is added to the mix.

The majority of scientists believe that different species did not originate all at once but at different times over a long period of time. They also believe that the first forms of life originated in the sea and that all subsequent forms of life "evolved." This is not consistent with the order in Genesis.

So how can these two accounts be reconciled? They **cannot** from the perspective of creation vs. evolution. The shortcomings of evolutionary theories, based on fossil evidence, will be discussed later. But as to the **timing** of God's creative acts, the **fossil evidence** does provide significant evidence that all species were not created at the same time. Perhaps a summary of what we have already learned will help us have a better understanding of this issue:

+ The days of Genesis were apparently metaphors for **unknown** periods of time.
+ The "mists" apparently began when the earth was created and **overlapped** into the third day.
+ The sun, moon and stars, "made" on the fourth day, were apparently "created" **earlier**, on the first day.
+ The literal sequence and details of many other events in the Bible are often sacrificed for literary arrangement (such as the first appearance of the rainbow, previously discussed).

Taking these things as a whole, it seems plausible that the events described for the first four days in the first chapter of Genesis, like many other things throughout the Scriptures, reflect a literary arrangement that is representative rather than all-inclusive. But, **had it not been for related Scriptures,** we would not have known this literary license was used. This is an extremely important finding because, unlike the creation of non-living

matter, **there are no other Scriptures to shed light on the creation of life
forms!** If there were, there is every reason to expect enlightenment as pro-
found as what we learned about the events of the first four days. Without
that enlightenment, how is it possible to know, with Scriptural certainty,
the exact order and timing of the creation of "all" of the various kinds of veg-
etable and animal life? Especially when we know that literary arrangement
often takes precedence over a literal sequence of events. And that the
Genesis account is so generic that it is not even representative of many
"kinds."

For example, nothing is said about the creation of vegetation that does
not produce "seeds." And many "seed-bearing plants and trees" (Genesis 1:11)
require pollination by a type of animal life not mentioned anywhere in the
Genesis account. A fact of nature that would lead us to conclude that some
kinds of animals, such as bees, were created **concurrently** with the "fruit
trees" **prior** to the mention of any kind of animal life. Countless "kinds" of
both animals and vegetables depend on this **balance of nature** for survival.

Another example of things that make it difficult to develop absolutes
from what has been revealed is the role of carnivorous animals. We can be
certain that man was originally prohibited from eating meat. But did this
extend to the animal kingdom as well?

> *Then God said, "I give you every seed-bearing plant on the face of the
> whole earth and every tree that has fruit with seed in it. They will be
> yours for food. And to all the beasts of the earth and all the birds of
> the air and all the creatures that move on the ground—everything
> that has the breath of life in it—I give every green plant for food"*
> (Genesis 1:29-30).

> *But after the flood God said to Noah, "Everything that lives and
> moves will be food for you. Just as I gave you the green plants, I now
> give you everything"* (Genesis 9:3).

Does this mean that beasts and birds were also restricted to a vegetar-
ian diet? If so, it wouldn't be long, as every farmer knows, before Adam
would be knee-deep in rabbits, mice, locusts and other fast-breeding
species that would have stripped the land of all vegetation. In short, if the

carnivorous food chain did not exist, there wouldn't be any vegetation for Adam and his descendants to eat. There is absolutely nothing in the fossil record or common knowledge that would lend credence to a world without the **balance of nature!** It is surely hard to look at the offensive and defensive structures of countless carnivores, both living and extinct, and conclude they were designed to eat grass and leaves:

> *The geological evidence of the existence of death in prehistoric times is…too powerful to be resisted…Perhaps the most that can be safely concluded from the language is "that it indicates merely the general fact that the support of the whole animal kingdom is based on vegetation"* (Dawson). (The Pulpit Commentary, Exposition).

This comment on Genesis 1:29-30 is given a lot of credibility by the fact that the prohibition on eating meat was lifted only for Noah and the human family. If the prohibition also applied to the animal kingdom in Genesis 1:29-30, and was not lifted in Genesis 9:3 or anywhere else in the Bible, when did they start eating each other? Some have assumed it was after Adam and Eve sinned. But this is only an assumption. Moreover, if all the earth were initially a paradise, why is it that God separated Adam from it and placed him in a specially prepared garden? Why would He do this if the environment outside the garden were no different than the inside?

> *Now the LORD God had planted a garden in the east, in Eden; and there he put the man he had formed. And the LORD God made all kinds of trees grow out of the ground—trees that were pleasing to the eye and good for food* (Genesis 2:8-9).

Another consideration is that it was God Himself who showed Adam and Eve that clothing made of animal skins was preferable to fig leaves (Genesis 3:21). We must either believe that clothing could only be obtained from an animal that died naturally or that God was teaching them to kill a lower level species to supply a higher level need. The latter seems more likely and is but another example where it seems the Scriptures, when referring to the diet of animals, were, like so many other things in the first chapter of

Genesis, written in generalities rather than all-inclusive absolutes—especially when we know that Abel, prior to lifting the prohibition on eating meat in the time of Noah, in obedience to God's commandment, killed animals as an act of worship (Genesis 4:4; Hebrews 11:4).

It would seem that the food chain of both life and death was a part of God's original laws of nature. Otherwise even the human population would, through procreation (Genesis 1:28), have eventually run out of room and sustenance. Even more to the point is what God said: "The man has now become like one of us, knowing good and evil. He must not be allowed to reach out his hand and take also from the tree of life and eat, and live forever" (Genesis 3:22). To "eat and live forever" **would have required an overt act by Adam!** Obviously, he was not physically designed to be eternal. How, then, did his sin bring "death" into the world?

> *Nevertheless, death reigned from the time of Adam to the time of Moses, even over those who did not sin*[16] *by breaking a command, as did Adam, who was a pattern of the one to come* (Romans 5:13-14).

> *I declare to you, brothers, that flesh and blood cannot inherit the kingdom of God, nor does the perishable inherit the imperishable* (1 Corinthians 15:50).

> *Dear friends, now we are children of God, and what we will be has not yet been made known. But we know that when he appears, we shall be like him, for we shall see him as he is* (1 John 3:2).

> *To him who overcomes, I will give the right to eat from the tree of life, which is in the paradise of God* (Revelation 2:7).

These Scriptures give strong testimony that sin itself did not change Adam's body from immortal to mortal. If sin is what causes a biological

---

16. In an earlier chapter (Romans 3:23), Paul said, "All have sinned and fall short of the glory of God." Who, then, are those who have not sinned? There is no universal theological agreement. Perhaps the answer lies in these three Scriptures: "Everyone who sins breaks the law" (1 John 3:4-5); "I would not have known what sin was except through the law" (Romans 7:7); "The little ones that you said would be taken captive, your **children who do not yet know good from bad**—they will enter the land" (Deuteronomy 1:39).

change in the body why would those "who did not sin" have died? Neither is it the "flesh and blood" of Adam's descendants that inherit the "right to eat from the tree of life" but those who have been given a new "imperishable" body "like" that of Jesus. What that body will look like "has not yet been made known."

It was his banishment from the Garden of Eden that brought physical death to Adam and his descendants, being **deprived of access** to the "tree of life." It is the reason God placed a cherubim "to guard the way to the tree of life" (Genesis 3:24). It is in obedience to Christ that this right of access, in a spiritual sense, is restored, "For since death came through a man, the resurrection of the dead comes also through a man. For as in Adam all die, so in Christ all will be made alive (1 Corinthians 15:21-23). As a point of interest, the Bible does not tell us when the Garden of Eden, guarded by a "cherubim," ceased to be a geographical landmark. Perhaps the Great Flood?

Another example of generalities used in the account of creation is that the unseen world of microscopic bacteria, essential for both vegetative and animal life, are not mentioned at all. This and the other things discussed should help us understand that there are lots of **details** about creation God chose not to reveal to the ancient Israelites:

> *My thoughts are not your thoughts, neither are your ways my ways declares the LORD. As the heavens are higher than the earth, so are my ways higher than your ways and my thoughts than your thoughts* (Isaiah 55:8-10).

> **The secret things belong to the LORD** *our God, but the things revealed belong to us and to our children forever, that we may follow all the words of this law* (Deuteronomy 29:29).

In line with this, **I am the first to acknowledge** that what I have presented as a possibility for the timing and sequence of some "kinds" of living things is done so with the utmost fear and reverence. I have filled in blanks without the kind of Scriptural enlightenment provided for the earlier, inanimate part of the creative week. Even that contains some subjective judgment. It is certain then that my opinion as to the possibilities for the latter part of the week is just that—an **opinion!**

But I am convinced that, unless one accepts the theology that the creative period was six literal days, there are simply too many unanswered questions to declare the first chapter of Genesis a complete account of when "all" species were created. There is certainly no basis to declare it to be in conflict with the fossil record—a record that is as much a testimony of God's creative activities as anything we may learn from the Scriptures. As we ponder the issue of creation, both scientifically and theologically, the only thing that seems abundantly clear is that each question only leads us into deeper and darker shades of ignorance.

Another issue that has been often raised, because of its possible impact on the reliability of the geological timetables, is the extent of the Great Flood. Was it universal or limited? The Bible says that "all" non-marine creatures were destroyed, indicating a worldwide flood (Genesis 7:21-22). **It may have been!** The text seems to indicate this to be the case. But why would God do this? He destroyed man because of sin. What motive would there have been for Him to destroy all living animals, which are incapable of sin, living in areas unpopulated by human beings?

The fact that God said he would destroy "all" may have been nothing more than a commonly used hyperbolic expression which, we already know, has been used in other parts of the Bible. As another example, "all the earth" (1 Kings 10:24) and "every creature under the heavens" (Colossians 1:23) are expressions that, in and of themselves, mean everyone on earth. In fact, the reference in Colossians, if taken literally, would mean the gospel was preached to every non-human "creature" as well ("anything created," Thayer's Greek Lexicon).

When God brought the plagues on Egypt, one of them destroyed "all" the livestock of the Egyptians (Exodus 9:5). Yet, in the very next plague, "festering boils broke out on men and animals" (Exodus 9:10). We also know that some of the Egyptians still had "livestock" when another plague occurred (Exodus 9:20-25). Does any of this mean that the Bible is incorrect in what is recorded? Is it possible that the plagues did not even occur? Of course not! Moses was simply using a **culturally correct, hyperbolic expression** to indicate widespread damage.

Another example is when Daniel, in interpreting a dream for the king of Babylon, told him of "a third kingdom, one of bronze, [which] will rule over the whole earth" (Daniel 2:39). This kingdom, which many Bible scholars believe to be that of Alexander the Great, did not rule the "whole earth."

That much of the animal population may have been spared during the flood is also given some credibility by the dispersion of different and often unique species to particular parts of the world, such as Australia and isolated islands. Also, if the entire earth experienced the same cataclysmic event, why is it that we do not find reasonably uniform sedimentary deposits throughout the world? On the other hand, there are things about the earth's layering of rocks that could certainly be interpreted as evidence for a worldwide, cataclysmic event such as the flood.

Whether God confined the flood to those areas inhabited by man or made it completely universal is not known. Speculation, of course, will never end. Even as this book is being written, scientists are finding evidence of an enormous flood that occurred about seven thousand years ago— apparently occasioned, at least in part, by the ocean breaking forth and flooding the Black Sea, turning it from fresh to salt water, and covering an enormous area of dry land. Many are beginning to wonder if this was the flood referred to in the book of Genesis. Such speculation does not explain forty days and nights of rain. And it certainly does not provide any human experience that would explain how the ark could have survived the sudden onslaught of a flash flood of ocean water several hundred feet high—or water deep enough to cover the tops of mountains.

Whatever one may believe about the flood, either scenario, localized or worldwide, defies common laws of hydrology. One would have held the waters in a particular area. The other would have required an amount of rain at the rate of as much as thirty feet an hour, nonstop, for almost a thousand hours, over the entire earth. Perhaps the scriptural evidence most often cited to support a local theory is the element involved besides the rain:

In the six hundredth year of Noah's life, on the seventeenth day of the second month—on that day all the springs of the great deep burst forth, and the floodgates of the heavens were opened. And rain fell on the earth forty days and forty nights (Genesis 7:11-12).

Of what benefit is the "springs of the great deep burst[ing] forth" if the whole earth was to be covered with water? A displacement of ocean water from one part of the earth to another would have neither increased nor decreased the need for additional water.

Both possibilities, local and worldwide, have their supporters and critics. But to insist on either interpretation neither recognizes the Bible usage of hyperbolic expressions nor the imposing and unlimited power of God. This is the same God who created the heavens and the earth (Genesis 1:1); made the sun go backward (Isaiah 38:8) and stand still (Joshua 10:12-13); divided the sea so the Israelites could cross on dry ground (Exodus 14:21-22); made the Jordan River stand up (Joshua 3:13); and calmed a raging storm with three words, "Quiet! Be still!" (Mark 4:39).

Now, having pointed out some of the Scriptural difficulties with a creation model of six, twenty-four hour days, we must also be aware that no explanation is without difficulties—**including the possibilities previously considered!** For while it appears, from both the Biblical account and scientific data, that the heavens and earth are much older than six thousand years, we cannot be certain that the earth was created millions or even billions of years ago. Why? Because the entire argument for such enormous ages, from a scientific point of view, is based on the **assumption** of "uniformitarianism," a theory that geological processes in the past were the same as they are now. Based on this assumption, scientists developed the "geological column" for assigning periods of time to the earth and fossil remains, such as the Mesozoic era ranging from seventy to two hundred million years ago, the era of the dinosaurs. One observation puts this entire issue into perspective:

> *The accuracy and significance of any or all such measurements are of course based entirely upon the accuracy with which the measurements can be made and the* **assumptions** *which enter into their interpretation. Far too little account has been taken of the* **limitations** *which these factors impose* (John C. Whitcomb and Henry M. Morris, The Genesis Flood, Baker Book House, Grand Rapids, Michigan, page 333, emphasis added).

The "measurements" referred to are such things as the process by which uranium and thorium disintegrate into lead and potassium into calcium and argon gas. Every such method ignores the fact that God perhaps, in the very beginning, created a universe containing lead, potassium, uranium, and all other elements in a state of harmonious completeness—**a universe of apparent age!**

A simple illustration brings this into sharp focus. Suppose Adam, the day after he was created, was examined by a panel of the world's best doctors. Would they not declare him to be an adult male, at least twenty years old, in perfect health, with all body parts functioning in complete harmony? Why should it be otherwise for the universe? Whatever one may believe about age-determining methods it is sheer nonsense to ignore this logical conclusion. How, then, can anyone living today determine the age of something that perhaps **began** in a state that would normally require an enormous amount of time to accomplish?

The difficulty of determining even more immediate prehistoric age is further illustrated by the fact that the very person who developed the commonly recognized Carbon 14 method of dating, W. F. Libby, was "shocked" to find that **he could not independently verify its accuracy** beyond a few thousand years:

> *The first shock Dr. Arnold and I had was that our advisors informed us that history extended back only 5000 years. We had thought initially that we would be able to get samples all along the curve back to 30,000 years, put the points in, and then our work would be finished. You read books and find statements that such and such a society or archaeological site is 20,000 years old. We learned rather abruptly that these numbers, these ancient ages, are not known; in fact, it is at about the time of the first dynasty in Egypt that the last historical date of any real certainty has been established* (W. F. Libby: "Radiocarbon Dating," American Scientist, volume 44, January 1956, page 107).

> *In order that a technique or discipline may be useful in scientific work, its limits must be known and understood, but the limits of usefulness of the radiocarbon age determinations are not yet known or understood.*

No one seriously proposes that all the determined dates are without error, but we do know how many of them are in error—25%? 50%? 75%? And we do not know which dates are in error, or by what amounts, or why. (Charles B. Hunt: "Radiocarbon Dating in the Light of Stratigraphy and Weathering Processes," *Scientific Monthly*, Volume 81, November 1955, page 240.)

In appraising C 14 dates, it is essential always to discriminate between the C 14 age and the actual sample. The laboratory analysis determines only the amount of radioactive carbon present...the laboratory analysis does not determine whether the radioactive carbon is all original or is in part secondary, intrusive, or whether the amount has been altered in still other irregular ways besides natural decay (Ernst Antevs: "Geological Tests of the Varve and Radiocarbon Chronologies," *Journal of Geology*, March 1957, page 129).

That these problems are still present is illustrated by disagreement in the scientific community about the Shroud of Turin. Initially, C 14 dating showed it to be less than a thousand years old. But other scientists felt the dating was tainted by "intrusive" elements. Perhaps one of the best resources for an in-depth study of different scientific points of view and inherent difficulties in determining the age of the earth is The Institute for Creation Research, El Cajon, California. Another source is a Christian book store where you can select from dozens of titles that address this issue in considerable detail.

But undoubtedly the most extensive and widely publicized criticism of commonly held scientific theories is *The Genesis Flood*, a book written by John C. Whitcomb and Henry M. Morris, published by Baker Book House, Grand Rapids, Michigan. This book examines and exposes, in great detail, some extremely difficult issues that the scientific community has not been able to answer or dismisses with inadequate postulations. I do not agree with several things in this book, but I recommend it as a resource that everyone should read who seeks a more comprehensive understanding of the "age" issue. A few quotations from the authors, and some from those they are quoting, show just how difficult it is to determine what happened in the past:

This is the great underlying principle of modern geology and is known as the principle of uniformitarianism...Without the principle of uniformitarianism there could hardly be a science of geology that was more than pure description (W. D. Thornbury, op. Cit., pp. 16, 17).

This principle is commonly stated in the Huttonian catchword that "the present is the key to the past." That is, geomorphic processes which can be observed in action at present, such as erosion, sedimentation, glaciation, volcanism, diastrophism, etc.—all operating in essentially the same fashion as at present—can be invoked to explain the origin and formation of all the earth's geologic deposits...But historical geology is unique among the sciences in that it deals with events that are past, and therefore not reproducible...it thus is impossible ever to prove that they were brought about by the same processes of nature that we can measure at present.

The only chronometric scale applicable in geologic history for the stratigraphic classification of rocks and for dating geological events exactly is furnished by the fossils (O. H Schindewolf: "Comments on Some Stratigraphic Terms," *American Journal of Science* [vol. 255, June 1957], page 394).

Paleogeography is anything but an exact science, largely owing to our limited knowledge but also to subjective interpretation, and moreover, there is also the danger of circular argument, since the geography of these early times is based at least in part on the distribution and supposed habitat of the very fossils with which we are dealing" (E. I. White, "Original Environment of the Craniates," in *Studies on Fossil Vertebrates*, edited by T. S. Westoll, London, Athlone Press, 1958).

It cannot be denied that from a strictly philosophical standpoint geologists are here arguing in a circle. The succession of organisms has been determined by a study of their remains embedded in the rocks, and the relative ages of the rocks are determined by the remains of organisms that they contain (R. H. Rastall, "Geology" in *Encyclopedia Brittannica*, 1956, page 168, volume 10).

*Does our time scale, then partake of Natural law? No...I wonder
how many of us realize that the time scale was frozen in essentially its
present form by 1840? How much world geology was known in 1840?
A bit of Western Europe, none too well, and a lesser fringe of eastern
North America. All of Asia, Africa, South America, and most of
North America were virtually unknown. How dared the pioneers
assume their scale would fit the rocks in these vast areas, by far most
of the world? Only in dogmatic assumption—a mere extension of the
kind of reasoning developed by Werner from the facts in his little dis-
trict of Saxony. And in many parts of the world, notably India and
South America, it does not fit. But even there it is applied! The followers of the founding fathers went forth across the earth and in
Procrustean fashion made it fit the sections they found, even in places
where the actual evidence literally proclaimed denial. So flexible and
accommodating are the "facts" of geology* (Edmund M. Spieker:
"Mountain-Building Chronology and Nature of Geologic Time-Scale,"
Bulletin American Association of Petroleum Geologists, Volume 40, August 1956,
page 1803).

*All calculations of radiocarbon dates have been made on the assumption
that the amount of atmospheric carbon dioxide has remained constant.
If the theory presented here of carbon dioxide variations in the atmosphere is correct, then the reduced carbon dioxide amount at the time of
the last glaciation means that all radiocarbon dates for events before the
recession of the glaciers are in question* (Gilbert N. Plass:"Carbon Dioxide
and the Climate," American Scientist, volume 44, July 1956, page 314).

*Similar calculations could be made for cobalt and other important
constituents of meteorites, all testifying that there simply cannot have
been meteoritic dust falling on the earth at present rates throughout
any five billion years of geologic time!*

*But if present processes cannot be used to deduce the earth's past his-
tory (and this fact is proved not only by the failure of geological uni-
formity but even more by the impregnable laws of conservation and
deterioration of energy), then the only way man can have certain*

knowledge of the nature of events on earth prior to the time of the beginning of human historical records, is by means of divine revelation. And this is why the Bible record of Creation and the Flood immediately becomes tremendously pertinent to our understanding, not only of the early history of the earth but also of the purpose and destiny of the universe and of man.

These quotations from *The Genesis Flood*, a large and comprehensive analysis of commonly held "age" theories, make it very difficult to ignore the following facts:

+ **Dating technologies are "helpless" unless proved by independent verification.**
+ **Independent verification "is not possible" for pre-historical time frames.**
+ **Geologic time and the ages of fossils are based on "circular reasoning." That is, the fossils are dated using geologic time and geologic time is dated using the fossils.**

A creation of apparent age and the circular reasoning and mental paradigms afflicting the scientific community provide valid reasons to suspect a high degree of error in determining the age of the earth and fossil remains. The geological time scale, essentially set in concrete by 1840 when world geology was in its infancy, remains the standard of time even though subsequent knowledge has proved its underlying assumptions were wrong. If age theories cannot be proven, where is the "science" in declaring the universe or any part of it, including animal life, to be any given age beyond recorded history? This does not mean such theories are completely wrong. But it does mean **they cannot be proven beyond some degree of doubt!**

In the first part of this chapter, I presented a correlation of the Biblical account of creation with the view that it was not in disharmony with an "old" earth. I based this correlation on the parallel accounts of creation in the books of Genesis and Proverbs and other Scriptures related to the creation process. But I then purposely exposed the acknowledged difficulties encountered by the scientific community in dating the earth and the possibility that the earth is much younger than commonly believed. I did this because, like most extremely difficult issues, the truth undoubtedly lies somewhere between the extreme and unyielding "positions" of many scientists and theologians who think they have it all figured out. For whatever one may choose to believe about time and sequence, creation processes, to say the least, are a mystery! **No theory, religious or scientific, is free from legitimate criticism!**

To that end, I urge everyone to be extremely careful in declaring an infallible religious doctrine on issues of science. Luther, Augustine and a host of other theologians, who are not scientists, have made that mistake time and time again. We should never again make the same mistake, as did Bryan in the Scopes trial, of diminishing the credibility of the Scriptures by trying to use them as a textbook in a debate on the details of physical and biological sciences. This is not to say he was wrong in much of what he said. He just used the wrong "proof." Had he relied more on the fossil record instead of the book of Genesis, evolutionary naturalism may very well have become only a footnote in biological textbooks. **Be careful of what you cannot prove!**

If ever there were "secret things [which] belong to the LORD our God" (Deuteronomy 29:29), it is the exact order, timing and processes of creation, especially when these things are identified as **mysteries known only by the God of creation** (Job 38:1-42:6). When he presumed too much, and God rebuked him by referring to these mysteries, Job replied, **"Surely I spoke of things I did not understand, things too wonderful for me to know"** (Job 42:3). As King David said, "I praise you because I am fearfully and wonderfully made; your works are wonderful (Psalm 139:14). Such are the sentiments everyone should have about all of God's creation. I would certainly be ill prepared to stand before the God of Judgment and explain how I compromised the "unsearchable riches of Christ" (Ephesians 3:8) to win an argument over "things too wonderful for me to know," whether it be of genealogies about geology, biology, or the Law of Moses:

> But avoid foolish controversies and genealogies and arguments and quarrels about the law, because these are unprofitable and useless. Warn a divisive person once, and then warn him a second time. After that, have nothing to do with him. You may be sure that such a man is warped and sinful; he is self-condemned (Titus 3:9-11).

It is better to know the rock of ages than the ages of rocks (Zingers, by Croftin Pentz, Tyndals House Publishers).

As we increase our understanding of the fossil record, genetic codes, the heavens above, and this unique blue planet God called "earth," we are reminded of the age-old maxim, "The more we learn the less we know." No one knows this better than scientists who are continually being forced to discard one theory after another. And, through honest reflection, they cannot help but recognize the enormous and incomprehensible intelligence and nature of the God who "created." For when all is said and done, and after we have learned all we can about the universal laws of nature that operate more precisely than a computer, we will still be left with the awesome reality that **someone beyond our plane of existence wrote the programs!**

The same can be said of theologians who, through new insights into ancient cultures and languages and the revelations of science, are being constantly overwhelmed by the unimaginable extent of the kingdom over which God made us rulers—the "fish of the sea and the birds of the air and over every living creature that moves on the ground" (Genesis 1:28). And whether our knowledge and instructions are derived from the pulpit or from the laboratory, each of us has the moral obligation to translate words into action to protect these creatures, to use whatever legitimate resources are available to us to not only protect life, but also this cherished and precious gift from God—the "heavens and the earth." He made us "rulers" over a creation that was "very good!" So far, to our shame, we have been extremely poor stewards. It is ironic that one of those whom white religionists considered "ignorant" and in need of "enlightenment" had a far better understanding of how we should view the earth:

I never said the land was mine to do with it as I chose. The one who has the right to dispose of it is the one who has created it (Chief Joseph of the Nez Perces, whose real name is Hinmahtooyahlatkekht, Thunder Rolling in the Mountains).

So it is written:

"The first man Adam became a living being"

1 Corinthians 15:45

CHAPTER FOUR

The Genesis Account of Man

MAN IS A UNIQUE CREATION! THERE IS NOTHING LIKE MODERN humans. Physically, we are just animals—unique to be sure, mentally transcending any other creature, but still an animal, sharing common DNA strings to a greater or lesser extent with other living creatures. But within man there is a spiritual consciousness, a craving, a compulsion to worship. We cannot help seeking the supernatural. It is an emotional need! No wonder! We alone have been created in the image of the Living God:

> Then God said, "Let us make man in our image, in our likeness, and let them rule over the fish of the sea and the birds of the air, over the livestock, over all the earth, and over all the creatures that move along the ground." So God created man in his own image, in the image of God he created him; male and female he created them (Genesis 1:26-27).

Though housed in a physical body this "image," this "likeness," is a spiritual attribute—"God is not a man...God is spirit" (Numbers 23:19; John

4:24). When we die, "the dust returns to the ground it came from, and the spirit returns to God who gave it...if the earthly tent we live in is destroyed, we have a building from God, an eternal house in heaven" (Ecclesiastes 12:7; 2 Corinthians 5:1).

But when did it start? When did man first appear? There is sharp disagreement between most scientists and theologians as to how long mankind has been on the earth. There is even disagreement within the religious community itself. The genealogical record of the Bible, taken as all-inclusive, indicates about six thousand years. But is this record all-inclusive? Does it provide all chronological details? A careful examination of the Bible itself teaches otherwise:

> *A record of the genealogy of Jesus Christ the son of David, the son of Abraham: ...Thus there were fourteen generations in all from Abraham to David, fourteen from David to the exile to Babylon, and fourteen from the exile to the Christ* (Matthew 1:1, 17).

As here, the Bible often applies the term "son" to any descendant, regardless of the length of time involved. David is not the "son" of Abraham. Jesus is not the "son" of David. They are fourteen generations apart. Even the "fourteen" is not correct. In Matthew's detailed listing by name of each group of fourteen, Ahaziah, Joash and Amaziah were omitted. Matthew knew this. It's just that his desire to achieve comparable groupings or literary arrangement was more important to him than absolute completeness about details. The same linguistic idiom of generation omissions also occurred in the book of Ezra:

> *After these things, during the reign of Artaxerxes king of Persia, Ezra son of Seraiah, the son of Azariah, the son of Hilkiah, the son of Shallum, the son of Zadok, the son of Ahitub, the son of Amariah, the son of Azariah, the son of Meraioth, the son of Zerahiah, the son of Uzzi, the son of Bukki, the son of Abishua, the son of Phinehas, the son of Eleazar, the son of Aaron the chief priest* (Ezra 7:1-5).

Adam Clark, an internationally respected Bible scholar, along with the commentator for the New International Version (NIV) of the Bible lend their insight to the cultural idioms of Hebrew writers based on this account in Ezra:

> *In this place there are only sixteen generations reckoned between Ezra and Aaron, but in (1 Chronicles 6:3-4), etc., there are not less than twenty-two. We must therefore supply the deficient generations from the above place, between Amariah son of Meraioth, (1 Chronicles 6:7), and Azariah the son of Johanan, (1 Chronicles 6:10). There are other discrepancies relative to genealogies in these historical books which it would be useless to investigate. On these differences much has been already said in different parts of this comment* (Adam Clark Commentary).

> *Seraiah was the high priest under Zedekiah who was killed in 586 [B.C.] by Nebuchadnezzar (2 Kings 25:18-21) some 128 years before Ezra's arrival. He was therefore the ancestor rather than the father of Ezra; "son" often means "descendant"* (NIV comment).

On another occasion, God said to Hezekiah that his sons would be carried away to Babylon, "Your own flesh and blood that will be born to you" (2 Kings 20:18). This did not happen to his immediate children, those "born" to him. It was several generations before this occurred. Such cultural idioms of expression ignore and discount the value of recording intervening events. There can be little doubt such thinking left out untold generations when the genealogical records of Genesis were written about the descendants of Noah:

> *This is the account of Shem, Ham and Japheth, Noah's sons, who themselves had sons after the flood. The sons of Japheth: Gomer, Magog, Madai, Javan, Tubal, Meshech and Tiras...These are the clans of Noah's sons, according to their lines of descent, within their nations. From these the nations spread out over the earth after the flood* (Genesis 10:1-32).

This chapter records a long listing of names for each son and their descendants. For the sake of brevity, the entire chapter was not quoted. But it is apparent from the following comments that the record does not give the complete picture of human genealogy:

Moses does not always give the name of the first settler in a country, but rather that of the people from whom the country afterward derived its name. Thus, Mizraim is the dual of Mezer, and could never be the name of an individual. The like may be said of Kittim Dodanim, Ludim, Ananim, Lehabim, Naphtuhim, Pathrusim, Casluhim, Philistim, and Caphtorim, which are all plurals, and evidently not the names of individuals, but of families or tribes. See (Genesis 10:4,6,13-14)…Moses also, in this genealogy, seems to have introduced even the name of some places that were remarkable in the sacred history, instead of the original settlers. Such as Hazarmaveth, (Genesis 10:26); and probably Ophir and Havilah, (Genesis 10:29). But this is not infrequent in the sacred writings, as may be seen (1 Chronicles 2:51), where Salma is called the father of Bethlehem, which certainly never was the name of a man, but of a place sufficiently celebrated in the sacred history; and in (Genesis 4:14), where Joab is called the father of the valley of Charashim, which no person could ever suppose was intended to designate an individual, but the society of craftsmen or arti-ficers who lived there (Adam Clark Commentary).

In the interpretation of the names which are here recorded, it is obvi-ously impossible in every instance to arrive at certainty, in some cases the names of individuals being mentioned, while in others it is as con-spicuously those of peoples (The Pulpit Commentary, Exposition).

These and preceding comments make it abundantly clear that the genealogies of Genesis, chapter 10, do not necessarily provide an immedi-ate father-to-son relationship. Another compelling reason to doubt that the Biblical timeline provides exact information is the manner in which a son of prominence is substituted for the firstborn son:

After Terah had lived 70 years, he became the father of Abram, Nahor and Haran…. Terah lived 205 years, and he died in Haran… (Genesis 11:26-32).

Abram was seventy-five years old when he set out from Haran…. After the death of his father (Genesis 12:4, Acts 7:4).

If Terah was 70 when Abram was born, how could Abram have been only 75 when he left Haran "after the death of his father," who died at the ripe old age of 205? Why would the writer say Abram was born when Terah was 70, but in the detail reveal a number that almost doubled Terah's age at the time of his birth (205—75 = 130)? What else could this be except a cultural idiom of expression that gave the father's age when his first son was born but substituted the name of the son of more importance? This was also done in the case of Shem and Japheth. Throughout the entire Bible, Shem is always listed first although Japheth is the older brother:

After Noah was 500 years old, he became the father of Shem, Ham and Japheth...Sons were also born to Shem, whose older brother was Japheth (Genesis 5:32; 10:21).

Another thing that calls into question the completeness of the genealogical record is found in Genesis 11:10-26, which lists the descendants of Shem to the time of Abraham. The following chart reflects the age of each father when the named son was born:

SON'S NAME	FATHERS AGE WHEN THE NAMED SON IS BORN
Arphaxad	2 years after the flood
Shelah	35
Eber	30
Peleg	34
Reu	30
Serug	32
Nahor	30
Terah	29
Abraham	<u>70</u>
Total	292 years

Noah was 600 years old at the time of the flood (Genesis 7:6). He died when he was 950 (Genesis 9:29). That's a difference of 350 years. If the records in Genesis, chapters 10 and 11, were all-inclusive, an exact timeline without any generation gaps, then Noah, patriarch of the flood, would have overlapped the life of Abraham by at least 58 years. This seems rather odd since there is no mention of his burial, as there was for Abraham and Isaac (Genesis 9:28-29; 25:7-9; 35:28-29). This is especially remarkable since Noah was not only a righteous and revered ancestor but the central figure of the Flood, one of the greatest events in human history (Hebrews 11:7). It would be completely out of context to think that Noah, if he had been alive in the time of Abraham, would have been buried without so much as a comment about his burial. But, of course, we already know this timeline is not complete. Abraham was not born to Terah at the age of 70. It was 60 years later. We have no way of knowing how many others in these genealogical records fall into the same category:

> *The genealogies of Scripture must be regarded as abridged. God had no intention that they should be used for the construction of a chronology. So far as the Bible is concerned, the date of the creation of Adam and Eve may be many times earlier than Ussher supposed. While it is pure speculation at present to say that the human race is a hundred thousand years old, there is nothing in Scripture which forbids such an assumption. No proved or imagined antiquity of man can be too great to be accepted by Christians, since no fundamental doctrine is in any way involved* (Nelson, Byron C., *Before Abraham*, [Minneapolis: Augsburg Publishing House, 1948], page 16).

Even the great age of men who lived before Noah raises further questions about genealogies. Men's life spans remained pretty much the same from Adam (930 years) to Noah (950 years), but significantly less for Abraham (175 years). Yet the generations listed in the Bible from Adam to Noah (9) and Noah to Abraham (10) are about the same. Why such a dramatic change if all generations are included? Of course, no one knows why this enormous decrease in life span occurred at all. But it does provide another reason to show that **the genealogical lists in the Bible are significantly incomplete and lacking in other significant details!**[17]

---

17. Jude 14 identifies Enoch as the "seventh" from Adam, leading some to believe this indicates a complete genealogy of names. Yet there is no theological consensus as to why Jude even quoted from this document. Although it was accepted by many as a historical document, it apparently did not exist "until the first century B.C." (NIV comment) and was never part of the Old Testament. Whatever one may think about the inspiration behind it, usage of this quotation would have been no different than the skipping of generations just discussed. Jude's purpose in writing was not about genealogies (1 Timothy 3:4). It was about apostasy in the church.

Left without the ability to establish that God gave us a complete register of names or that the father/son birth dates are exact, we cannot, from the Scriptures, determine how long man has been on the earth. Neither can we determine when the flood occurred. However, there are things the Bible does say, **supported by the fossil record**, that negate the claim by many scientists that man "evolved" from an ancient creature that lived millions of years ago.

According to the Bible, Adam and Eve were not meat-eating savages with little more intellect than beasts of the field. They talked, reasoned and communed with God. They were horticulturists, responsible for maintaining the Garden of Eden. Once they had sinned and recognized their nakedness, they made clothing of fig leaves. Not for warmth, for they had been living without any clothing at all. It was a sense of shame, a sense of morality, which established the need to cover their nakedness. No other animal has ever shown such a trait.

Moreover, their firstborn son, Cain, was a farmer who, later in life, built a city. Their son Abel was a shepherd. Both worshipped and offered sacrifices to God. Some time after Cain murdered Abel he became a marked man in the eyes of other people. It is obvious from this that people, from the very beginning, valued and protected life by a moral code. Cain understood this:

> Cain said to the LORD, "My punishment is more than I can bear. Today you are driving me from the land, and I will be hidden from your presence; I will be a restless wanderer on the earth, and whoever finds me will kill me." But the LORD said to him, "Not so; if anyone kills Cain, he will suffer vengeance seven times over." Then the LORD put a mark on Cain so that no one who found him would kill him. So Cain went out from the LORD's presence and lived in the land of Nod, east of Eden. Cain lay with his wife, and she became pregnant and gave birth to Enoch…Adam lay with his wife again, and she gave birth to a son and named him Seth, saying, "God has granted me another child in place of Abel, since Cain killed him." …After Seth was born, Adam lived 800 years and had other sons and daughters (Genesis 4:13–5:4).

In an attempt to discount this Scriptural record is the question and comment, "How could Cain get a wife from Nod if the only other people were his parents? Seth had not yet been born when Cain mentioned other people." To get right to the point, **the Bible does not say** how long it was between Abel's death and the marriage of Cain. It could have easily been after Seth was born and had children. Each of these ancient people lived several hundred years—ample time to have produced several families through one or more of their sisters. Both polygamy (Genesis 4:19; 1 Kings 11:3) and marriage to a relative were consistent with common practices. Even Abraham, the revered ancestor of Jews, Christians and Moslems, married his half-sister and sought a relative, with God's help and approval, to become his son's wife (Genesis 20:12; 24:1-67).

It seems that much ado has been made about nothing. The only thing the Bible tells us is that "Cain...lived in the land of Nod...and lay with his wife, and she became pregnant" (Genesis 4:16-17). There is not one Scriptural reference that tells us where she came from. **Or when he married her!** All we know is that Cain obviously married a sister or a niece who either went with him into Nod or became his wife at a later date.

Neither do the Scriptures indicate there were any other people in "Nod" at all. In fact, the Hebrew word for "Nod" simply means "vagrancy" or "wandering." This is in harmony with the fact that Cain "built a city," **where one did not previously exist**, and named it after his son Enoch. The commonly perceived notion that Cain trotted over to an inhabited city and married one of the local women who was in no way related to him is pure imagination. **The text does not teach this!** Neither does the text give any comfort to those who would use it in a feeble attempt to advance the notion that this was Jewish mythology.

But what about those people Cain feared would kill him? It is only logical that Cain knew what God had told his parents, "Be fruitful and increase in number; fill the earth and subdue it" (Genesis 1:28). He also knew that these other descendants of Adam and Eve would be governed by a moral code, decreed by God, against murder. Why wouldn't he think they would kill him rather than let him live in their midst?

It should be obvious from all of this that Moses, as he did with creation, **ignored a lot of extraneous details!** Even today, many of us would have relayed the incidents in much the same way. Rather than break the story line about Cain, Abel and Seth, the writer simply chose to mention other sons and daughters and the land of Nod almost as a footnote or parenthetical remark. This is entirely consistent with the manner in which we are given some insight into the past through genealogical records that ignore exact timelines and events not essential to the record. No doubt this is why God tells us to avoid quibbling about such non-related events and details that do nothing but generate controversies (opinions) rather than issues of salvation (commands). Again, Paul's admonition:

> *As I urged you when I went into Macedonia, stay there in Ephesus so that you may command certain men not to teach false doctrines any longer nor to devote themselves to myths and endless genealogies. These promote controversies rather than God's work—which is by faith* (1 Timothy 1:3-4).

But some scientists doubt the Biblical record because of the remains of primitive people, "hunters and gatherers," whose spiritual nature leaves little doubt they were human. Does this prove they evolved from a lower level of animal? Why should it be thought improbable that they were displaced people, descendants of Noah, who, for any number of reasons, found themselves in a hostile environment where social and personal skills had to be significantly modified in order to survive? Even in this industrial age, we still have such groups in remote areas of the earth. Does this make these people less than any other modern humans—now or thousands of years ago? Bring the children from such groups, educate them in our ways, and they will become as much a part of our society as those born to the rich and powerful. **No other animal on earth possesses this unique capability!** Scientists have tried in vain to duplicate this trait in other animals. Every attempt has been a miserable failure.

This same adaptability also works in reverse. Remove any one of us to a place of primitive circumstances, where the law of the jungle is the only way to survive, and see how we live. In the jungle, where death lurks behind every bush and there are no tools and "how-to-do-it" manuals, the stock wizard from Wall Street would soon find that reversion to Maslow's lowest level of hierarchical survival needs is all that counts. We would adapt! We would become hunters and gatherers, using ancient stone tools as they did.

And if we died in that jungle and our remains and artifacts were found ten thousand years later, what would an archaeologist or paleontologist con- clude about our intellect? Would they not conclude we were primitive? Maybe even savages.

Which gives rise to the question, "Who is the savage?" The one who kills to survive or the one who destroys solely for economic or political gain? The one who uses a spear to protect his family or the one who invents bio- logical, chemical and nuclear arsenals capable of destroying the whole world? The one who adapts to the environment or the one who destroys entire ecological systems for a few years of use? Perhaps we are much like the people who built the tower of Babel. We have become too big for our own britches. Pollution and destruction of rain forests and the ozone layer are things even politicians can no longer ignore.

But there is one observation about the period between Adam and Noah that is inconsistent with what we presently know about the invention of metallurgy. According to the Bible such skills were known prior to the Great Flood, "Zillah also had a son, Tubal-Cain, who forged all kinds of tools out of bronze and iron" (Genesis 4:22). By any method of Biblical dat- ing this far precedes the first archaeological evidence of the use of such implements. Based on this, scientists find it difficult to accept the above statement as anything but Jewish mythology. Tragically, even some theolo- gians speculate that the text was developed as a part of Jewish lore by someone who had knowledge of bronze and iron, probably about 1000 B.C. But, again, we run into these mental paradigms that attempt to place limits on God. There is simply no way of knowing what happened before the Flood. God destroyed all human life. Why, then, should it seem unlikely that He also destroyed all evidence of human existence?

> So the LORD said, "I will wipe mankind, whom I have created, from the face of the earth" (Genesis 6:7).

In this state of mind, God is very capable of not only destroying the people in the Great Flood, but all evidence that the people ever existed. In fact, the Bible teaches this was not an unusual reaction of God when He chose, in His anger, to destroy everything that belonged to the people who incurred His wrath, to "cut off the memory of them from the earth." An act that would be contextually consistent with the purpose of the flood:

The LORD said to Moses and Aaron, "Separate yourselves from this assembly so I can put an end to them at once...then you will know that these men have treated the LORD with contempt." As soon as he finished saying all this, the ground under them split apart and the earth opened its mouth and swallowed them, with their households and all Korah's men and all their possessions. They went down alive into the grave, with everything they owned; the earth closed over them, and they perished and were gone from the community (Numbers 16:20-33).

Endless ruin has overtaken the enemy, you have uprooted their cities; even the memory of them has perished (Psalm 9:6).

The face of the LORD is against those who do evil, to cut off the memory of them from the earth (Psalm 34:16).

They are now dead, they live no more; those departed spirits do not rise. You punished them and brought them to ruin; you wiped out all memory of them (Isaiah 26:14).

In summary, the Bible teaches that God created man, fully formed and functional, with the knowledge to make clothing, farm and raise livestock, build cities, and live by a moral and spiritual code. It also teaches that man was the last and most recent creation, **a fact confirmed by both fossil and archaeological records!** But the Bible does not provide sufficient information to determine **when** that creation occurred, or **when** the Great Flood occurred that gave mankind a new beginning. These are just a couple of many things God has not revealed in the Scriptures. The most fundamental lesson to be learned about creation is that it is a mystery shrouded in the mists of the past. Everyone, however great and renowned, is still faced with the stark reality that:

- **EVERY THEOLOGICAL THEORY HAS GAPS AND INCONSISTENCIES.**
- **EVERY SCIENTIFIC THEORY HAS GAPS AND INCONSISTENCIES.**

    While Christians may have differences of opinion about the timing of creation, there should never be any doubt that it was Adam's divine creation "in the image of God," giving us the ability to love and care for the most unfortunate among us, that separated the human species from all others, a trait especially exhibited by those who have been "born again" (John 3:3-7; Acts 20:35; Romans 13:1-13; 15:1-2; Philippians 2:1-4; 1 Thessalonians 5:14-15):

The general scientific world has been bamboozled into believing that evolution has been proved. Nothing could be further from the truth.[18]

18. F. Hoyle & N. C. Wickramasinghe, *Evolution from Space*. Dent, London, 1981.

CHAPTER FIVE

Unrestricted Organic Evolution: Fact or Deception

RATIONALITY IS THE FIRST THING THAT GOES WHEN SOMEONE SUG-
gests we may be wrong about a cherished "position." Divorce courts have wit-
nessed some of the most intelligent and gentle people on earth becoming
completely irrational and vindictive. Religious people whose "doctrine" is challenged have often invented the most hideous of schemes to punish those who
disagreed with them, many of them doing so under the banner of Jesus Christ,
the "Prince of Peace." These mental paradigms of "position" completely blocked
their ability to be rational. It is an understatement to say that many scientists
are also afflicted with this paradigm when it comes to the subjects of creation
and evolution.

Over fifty years ago, Waldo Shumway of the University of Illinois said,
with respect to the theory of embryological recapitulation (also called the
"biogenetic law"), that a consideration of the results of experimental
embryology "seem to demand that the hypothesis be abandoned." Walter J.
Bock of the Department of Biological Sciences of Columbia University
later said:

> ...*the biogenetic law has become so deeply rooted in biological thought*
> *that it cannot be weeded out in spite of its having been demonstrated*
> *to be wrong by numerous subsequent scholars* (W. J. Bock, *Science*
> 164:684 [1969]).[19]

This is a prime example where mental paradigms of "position" block out rational thought. This may be expected from the religious community where emotion often plays a major part in belief systems. But it should not be so with scientists. They are trained to be objective. Yet it is apparent that many scientists have surely lost their sense of commitment to objectivity by clinging tenaciously to the theory of unlimited organic evolution in spite of genetic and fossil evidence to the contrary. Even worse, by its own definition, the theory excludes even the possibility of supernatural creation. Its fundamental doctrine is that "scientific laws can explain all phenomena" (*Webster's New Universal Unabridged Dictionary*).

This is a claim that is patently false and ignores what its own adherents know to be true. It is an open secret that scientists cannot even come close to explaining all phenomena. To illustrate the extent to which this "secret" has been kept from the masses of people, I have chosen quotations from scientists **throughout the entire twentieth century!** These scientists, quoted in this and other chapters, are some of the most highly respected researchers in the world.[20] They openly admit **they cannot avoid the creative implications of the sudden and unexplainable appearance of new species!** Species that are both unique and fully formed and functional **from their beginning!** And remain so, in all-essential aspects, as long as the species exist!

Forgetting about any particular religious doctrine, the physical evidence supports the fundamental belief by most people that "in the beginning" there was a God who "created." This is a finding reported by numerous surveys. It is a finding this author can verify. It is a rare thing to find someone who does not believe in a creative God. Why is this? Because common sense

---

19. Duane Gish, *Evolution: The Fossils Still Say No!* Institute for Creation Research, El Cajon, CA.
20. The impressive education and experience credentials of these scientists, though not listed in this or other chapters, are available at most public libraries. They are widely known men and women, eminently qualified to present the general beliefs of most paleontologists, anthropologists, physicists, biologists, geologists, mathematicians, astronomers and other scientific disciplines related to the subjects discussed.

tells us that by the laws of nature, to which we are bound, it is impossible for anything physical to exist. It doesn't take a degree in physics to know that, within the bounds of natural law, matter cannot just appear—**something cannot come from nothing! An absolute vacuum will forever remain an absolute vacuum!** It is only by "faith we understand that the universe was formed at God's command, so that what is seen was not made out of what was visible" (Hebrews 11:3).

There is simply no scientific way to explain the impossible. Scientists can only analyze what exists, what is possible within the parameters of nature! Moreover, in attempting to understand the past they are further limited to the use of present-day evidence. **They were not there in the past!** Were it not for fossils they would not know that dinosaurs once roamed the earth. Were it not for the current position and movement of stars they would have never been able to even speculate that the universe began with a "Big Bang!" Even if true, the scientific quagmire is no less formidable for those who deny the existence of God. **Where did the material come from to go "Bang"?**

If scientists cannot determine the source of matter, the source of energy, how can they go back even further and address the existence or non-existence of God, a supernatural power that exists beyond human limitations? Yet, in spite of this quandary, there are still some scientists and even others with less imposing credentials who proclaim loud and long, "There is no God," and refer to those who do as "ignorant" and "unlearned." But, at the end of the day, after all is said and done, everyone, from scientist to theologian to the man or woman on the street, is left with four inescapable conclusions:

+ **The universe and all its inhabitants exist!**
+ **No one can explain how it's possible for anything to exist!**
+ **No one can disprove the existence of a supernatural power!**
+ **How, when, and by whom the universe and its life forms began is a matter of faith!**

Why, then, is the idea of a creative, supernatural force we call God deemed to be in the realm of ignoramuses and unsuited for classroom possibilities? And why does the same reasoning not apply to the inhabitants of that universe? If God created the universe He could certainly create life. Where is the logic in admitting one and denying the other? Especially when the fossil evidence, the objective record of those life forms, shows that different species did not leave a chain of unbroken evolution. Rather, they just unexplainably and suddenly appeared and disappeared!—a fact that some of the most respected scientists in the world have acknowledged. Certain statements are highlighted to emphasize critical issues:

> ...*"creation," in the ordinary sense of the word is perfectly conceivable. I find no difficulty in conceiving that, at some former period, this universe was not in existence, and that it made its appearance in six days (or instantaneously, if that is preferred), in consequence of the volition of some preexisting Being. Then, as now, the so-called a priori arguments against Theism and, given a Deity, against the possibility of creative acts,* **appeared to me to be devoid of reasonable foundation** (T. H. Huxley, quoted in *Life and Letters of Thomas Henry Huxley*, volume I, editor L. Huxley [Macmillan, 1903], page 241).

> ...*there is the theory that all living forms in the world have arisen from a single source which itself came from an inorganic form. This theory can be called the "General Theory of Evolution" and* **the evidence that supports it is not sufficiently strong to allow us to consider it as anything more than a working hypothesis** (G. A. Kerkut, *Implication of Evolution* [New York: Pergamon Press, 1960], page 157).

> *Because understanding of the actual evolutionary events that took place over earth's long history depends largely on interpretations of an incomplete fossil record, much latitude remains for differences in such interpretations. One of the issues that is currently being debated among theorists derives from a notable fact observed in the fossil record; that is, when a new species appears in the record it usually does so abruptly and then apparently remains stable for as long as the record of that species lasts.* **The fossils do not seem to exhibit the slow and gradual changes that might be expected** (Evolution," Microsoft® Encarta. Copyright © 1994 Microsoft Corporation. Copyright © 1994 Funk & Wagnall's Corporation).

> *No matter how far back we go in the fossil record of previous animal life upon the earth we find no trace of any animal forms which are*

*intermediate between the various groups of phyla...**The greatest
groups of animal life do not merge into one another.** They are and
have been fixed from the beginning...No animals are known even
from the earliest rocks which cannot at once be assigned to their proper
phylum or major group...* (The New Evolution, Zoogenesis, Baltimore:
Williams and Wilkins, 1930, pages 129ff).

*So we see that the fossil record, the actual history of the animal life on
the earth, bears out the assumption that at its very first appearance
animal life in its broader features was essentially the same as that in
which we now know it...Thus, so far as concerns the major groups of
animals, the **creationists seem to have the better of the argument.**
There is not the slightest evidence that any of the major groups arose
from any other* (Quarterly Review of Biology, December, 1928, page 539).

*It has been argued that the series of paleontological finds is too inter-
mittent, too full of "missing links" to serve as a convincing proof. If a
postulated ancestral type is not found, it is simply stated that it has not
so far been found. Darwin himself often used this argument and in his
time it was perhaps justifiable. But it has lost its value through the
immense advances of paleobiology in the twentieth century...**The
true situation is that those fossils have not been found which were
expected.** Just where new branches are supposed to fork off from the
main stem it has been impossible to find the connecting types* (N.
Heribert-Nilsson: Synthetische Artbildung [Verlag CWH Gleerup,
1953], page 1188).

*Those opposed to creeping evolution point out, quite fairly, that most
species do not change at all through their evolutionary lifetimes, **which
is not what Darwin would have expected*** (Steve Jones, The Language
of Genes, Anchor Books, Bantam Doubleday Dell Publishing Group, Inc.,
1540 Broadway, New York, NY 10036, page 106).

***The fossil record does not convincingly document a single transition
from one species to another.** Furthermore, species lasted for astound-
ingly long periods of time* (The New Evolutionary Timetable, page 95).

Change is difficult and rare, rather than inevitable and contin-
ual...species within their own peculiar adaptations, behaviors, and
genetic systems are remarkably conservative, often remaining
unchanged for several million years (Roger Lewin, Bones of Contention,
Published by Simon & Schuster, Rockefeller Center 1230 Avenue of the
Americas, New York, NY, 10020, page 41).

Many biologists nowadays have doubts about Darwin's theory, and
think it might have to be modified. But there are other biologists who
go a great deal further, and think Darwinism is worthless. These are
not creationists. **They are evolutionists who consider that Darwin's**
theory cannot be made to fit the facts, no matter how much biolo-
gists might modify it. *Their view is that nothing less than an entirely*
new theory is needed to explain evolution. So far they have not man-
aged to find one, but they are still looking. There have long been quite
a number of these folk about. And those I shall quote in this chapter
are generally regarded as quite distinguished biologists, despite their
unorthodox view (Alan Howard, Creation and Evolution: Bethany House
Publishers, Minneapolis, Minnesota).

One by one the great prophets of materialism have been shown to be
false prophets and have fallen aside. Marx and Freud have lost their
scientific standing. **Now Darwin is on the block** (Phillip E. Johnson, J.
D., Professor of Law, University of Calif., in Mere Creation, InterVarsity
Press, Downers Grove, Ill., page 453).

The pattern that we were told to find for the last 120 years does
not exist (Natural History, "Evolutionary Housecleaning," by Niles
Eldridge, February 1982, page 81).

This text [a Darwinist book] suggests that modern bacteria are evolv-
ing very quickly, thanks to their innumerable mutations. **Now this is**
not true. *For millions, or even billions, of years, bacteria have not*
transgressed the structural frame within which they have always fluc-
tuated and still do... **To vary and evolve are two different things;**
this can never be sufficiently emphasized (P. P. Grasse, Evolution of Living
Organisms, Academic Press, New York & London, 1977, page 6).

Now we would like to pursue that inquiry farther back in time, but the barrier to further progress seems insurmountable. It is not a matter of another year, another decade of work, another measurement or another theory; **at this moment it seems as though science will never be able to raise the curtain on the mystery of creation.** *For the scientist who has lived by faith in the power of reason, the story ends like a bad dream. He has scaled the mountains of ignorance; he is about to conquer the highest peak; as he pulls himself over the final rock, he is greeted by a band of theologians who have been sitting there for centuries* (Robert Jastrow, *God and the Astronomers*, [New York: Warner Books, 1980], 104-6).

How can anyone read such statements and declare that "unlimited organic evolution is a fact"? Or that "scientific laws can explain all phenomena"? Change, of course, does occur—both naturally and when it is induced by human intervention. The natural world is filled with differences in body structure among particular kinds of animals, including the human family. But this is not evolution, as it is commonly understood, but controlled change, most often identified as microevolution, succession or variation. As Professor Grasse, one of the world's most distinguished biologists, said, "**To vary and evolve are two different things.**"

In summary, no one can scientifically demonstrate that the universe came into being other than from a source of power that humanity refers to as God. Neither has science been able to demonstrate from the fossil record that fully formed and fully functional vegetative and animal "kinds" came into being through evolution. Instead, scientists have found overwhelming testimony from the fossil record that each "kind" was uniquely created and then, by natural law, limited in the degree of change that subsequently occurred. This is not religious hocus-pocus. This is an acknowledgment, as you have already read, by renowned scientists.

Yet, in spite of this undeniable evidence, most evolutionary naturalists still persist in preaching the doctrine of unlimited evolution, more commonly known as Darwinism. Many of them also tend to look on the rest of us, as did Darwin, who said, "The stupidity of the human race never fails to surprise me." A statement reiterated by a current day Harvard professor:

It is infuriating to be quoted again and again by creationists—whether through design or stupidity, I do not know—as admitting that the fossil record includes no transitional forms. Transitional forms are generally lacking at the species level but are abundant between larger groups. The evolution from reptiles to mammals ...is well documented (Stephen Jay Gould, *Creation/Evolution*, 6 [Fall 1981], page 38).

So says Professor Gould, who may have good reason to be upset for having his quotes taken out of context. But to refer to those who challenge his interpretation of the fossil record as doing so out of "stupidity" seems rather harsh, especially when he is advocating a house without foundation. For if transitional fossil evidence is, in his own words, "generally lacking at the species level," the lowest level of classification, how can he say that transitional forms are "abundant between larger groups?" How, in the name of reason, could they just skip the lower groupings, the foundation on which all else depends? I may not be a scientist, but I know that a house is only as good as its foundation. And that an argument is only as good as its premise.

Professor Gould's antagonism and name calling is no doubt born out of frustration that his theories are simply contrary to what he had hoped the fossil record would reveal, but has not! Moreover, to be consistent, he would also have to classify many fellow scientists as being "stupid." As noted earlier, this phenomenon of missing fossils is now being seriously debated among scientists themselves, even by those who are still clinging to the possibility of evolution. Why this tenacious hold on the possibility of evolution? Because there is no alternative to evolution except **supernatural creation!**

In short, it is an indisputable fact that commonly espoused evolutionary theories are based on a lot of missing information—gaps in the fossil record that cry out for acceptance of a creative God rather than even an updated Darwinian doctrine. A comment by Dr. Homer W. Parker, Sr., whose writings reflect an avowed and uncompromising evolutionary mind set, illustrates this penchant for linguistic creativity when the fossils are missing:

Overall time, on these early fossils, is being found to be millions of year intervals. It could have initially evolved at another location earlier and what we have is merely a descendent (Dr. Homer W. Parker, Sr., *Evolution of Man Since The Earth Was Created*, page 65).

Dr. Parker has summed up the entire concept of evolutionary theories in two words. He said that new species "could have" descended from some previous life-form. The sum and substance of the evidence to support the doctrines taught in our school systems and educational media programs is that it "**could have**" happened. How can such theories be deemed more logical than a belief that God exists and that He used creative license to impose the basic composition of each species?

A scientific attempt to answer this embarrassment to evolutionary naturalism is called emergent or quantum evolution or punctuated equilibrium.[21] That is, life-forms that appear suddenly are derived in some "unexplainable" way from earlier forms of life or evolved so rapidly in isolated groups that they left few or no transitional fossils at the species level. However, a recognized authority on evolution, Julian Huxley, had this to say about the problem of circumventing genetic laws that limit change:

A proportion of favorable mutations of one in a thousand does not sound much, but is probably generous, since so many mutations are lethal, preventing the organism living at all, and the great majority of the rest throw the machinery slightly out of gear. And a total of a million mutational steps sound a great deal but is probably an underestimate...after all, that only means one step every two thousand years during biological time as a whole. However, let us take these figures as being reasonable estimates. With this proportion, but without any selection, we should clearly have to breed a million strains (a thousand squared) to get one containing two favorable mutations; and so on, up to a thousand to the millionth power to get one containing a million. Of course, this could not really happen, but it is a useful way of visualizing the fantastic odds against getting a number of favorable mutations in one strain through pure chance alone. A thousand to the millionth power, when written out, becomes the figure 1 with three million noughts after it: and that would take three large volumes of about five hundred pages each, just to print! Actually this is a meaninglessly large figure, but it shows what a degree of improbability natural selection has to surmount, can circumvent. One

---

21. Niles Eldridge, Ph.D., a curator in the Department of Invertebrates at the American Museum of Natural History in New York, along with Professor Stephen J. Gould, professor of zoology and geology at Harvard University, originated the idea of punctuated equilibrium.

with three million noughts after it is the measure of the unlikeliness of a
horse—the odds against it happening at all. No one would bet on any-
thing so improbable happening; and yet it has happened. It has hap-
pened, thanks to the workings of natural selection and the properties of
living substance which make natural selection inevitable (Huxley, Julian.
Evolution in Action, [New York: Harper and Brothers, 1953], pages 41, 42).

How can anyone reconcile Mr. Huxley's own statement, "it has happened," with his own perception of the facts? He himself acknowledged the
enormous degree of improbability of such evolution—"it could not really
happen"—"no one would bet on anything so improbable." To make such
statements and then conclude it "did happen" has to be a proclamation of
faith. Evolution has, **by any reasonable measure,** become his paradigm of
thought. For even on those rare occasions when permanent change occurs,
it tends to be minimal. Why? Because **species are genetically pro-
grammed to remain unchanged!**

When scientists ignore such imposing physical evidence for one side of
the equation and insist on theories that have very limited physical evidence
to support it, they have moved from the arena of science into the realm of
religious faith. **They have created an idol of the mind,** a god as real as
those made of "gold or silver or stone" (Acts 17:29). Lord Zuckerman essentially agreed when he said, concerning theories about the human family, it
is such "an incredibly difficult problem...that I think it would be legitimate
to despair that one could ever turn it into a science."[22] "The situation has
become so embarrassing to evolutionists that some seek to disavow the
importance of the fossil record to evolution theory. British zoologist and
evolutionist Mark Ridley is now claiming:"[23]

*The gradual change of fossil species has never been part of the evi-
dence for evolution...no real evolutionist...uses the fossil record as
evidence in favor of the theory of evolution as opposed to special creation* (M. Ridley, New Scientist 90:830 [1981]).

---

22. Choose Your Ancestors," Lecture at the California Institute of Technology, Pasadena,
September 1974.
23. Duane T. Gish, *Evolution: The Fossils Still Say No*; Institute for Creation Research, El Cajon,
CA, page 351-2.

This is acknowledgment by a devout evolutionist that the fossil record cries out for belief in a creative God. And that theories of evolutionary naturalism are based on subjective philosophy (**words**) rather than the only cold, hard evidence that exists—fossils that cry out for special creation. This dismissal of the fossil record by Ridley has been condemned by one of the most distinguished zoologists in the world:

> *Naturalists must remember that the process of evolution is revealed only through fossil forms ...Neither the examination of present beings, nor imagination, nor theories* **can serve as a substitute for paleontological documents** (P. Grasse, *Evolution of Living Organisms* [New York: Academic Press, 1977], page 4, emphasis supplied).

Even an abbreviated review of scientific journals and books, written by world-renowned scientists and authors, shows that **traditional evolutionary theories are based more on human inventiveness and self-imposed paradigms than actual fossil or genetic evidence!** There is far more fossil proof of a creative God than evolutionary theories that try in vain to explain away, without essential supporting evidence, **those missing links—** those immutable parameters which both vegetative and animal "kinds" **have not crossed!**

Of course, some scientists believe they have found one of the missing links between dinosaurs and birds (what happened to the "well documented" theory that they evolved into mammals? see page 126.) based on a fossil found in China, named *Archaeoraptor liaoningensis*, that appears to show a dinosaur with rudimentary feathers.[24]

But not all scientists are ready to jump to this conclusion. Larry D. Martin of the University of Kansas stated that "Archaeoraptor is one of the worst preserved specimens in a long line of poorly preserved specimens...the fossil appears to be a composite made by putting together pieces of two facing sides of a split slab—called part and counterpart by paleontologists."[25] In the same article, paleontologist Stephen Czerkas acknowledged that those who found the specimen "did glue together sections of the part and

---

24. *National Geographic Magazine*, November 1999.
25. *Science News*, November 20, 1999.

counterpart, but he argues the fossil is from one individual." He also reports finding, in Utah, an "impression of a tiny animal that appeared to have the feathers of a bird but the long, bony tail of a dinosaur."

One is a "composite" and the other "appeared" to possess these unusual characteristics. Even if these are legitimate fossil specimens, are they one of the missing links showing that genetic barriers have been crossed? Or does it mean scientists have simply discovered another rare creation, such as the platypus; a unique species that has the bill of a duck, lays leathery-shelled eggs like a reptile, and nurses its young like the true mammal it is. Because platypus is unique it was many years before the scientific community, as a whole, acknowledged that such a creature actually existed.

If, as speculated, there may have been as many as a billion different species, is it not likely that a few rare creatures with cross-species characteristics would have been created? Isn't it amazing that many scientists presume that God would be bound to some preordained logic of humanity. It is the **preponderance of evidence** that should sway the jury, not an extreme rarity that, as the platypus shows, is not only possible but actually happened. On the other hand you could, in spite of the evidence for special creation, believe what one well-known evolutionist has said, "The first bird hatched from a reptilian egg."[26] Such a statement illustrates the extremes to which evolutionary theorists feel they must go to explain away a fossil record that still says "NO!"[27] A record that says:

+ **CREATION IS BASED ON FOSSIL "EVIDENCE!"**
+ **EVOLUTION IS BASED ON "WORDS!"**

This chapter would not be complete without repeating an observation made in an earlier chapter about the **"balance of nature."** Every thinking person knows that a proper balance between plants and animals is absolutely essential to maintain life—**"living things depend on each other!"** (*World Book Encyclopedia*) This unassailable fact is the heart and soul of environmental laws. Whether or not "all" species were created at the same time is a legitimate issue for religious and scientific inquiry. But there

26. R. B. Goldschmidt, *The Material Basis of Evolution* (New Haven: Yale University Press, 1940, page 395.

27. Duane T. Gish, Ph. D., Biochemistry; *Evolution: The Fossils Still Say No.*

should be no question that, if there is any validity at all to the scientific view that the "present is the key to the past," many **interdependent species came into being at the same time! Fully developed and fully functional!**

Even the amazing ability of life-forms to adapt to different environments does not answer the question of the "time" and "circumstances" needed for development of unique and life-dependent functions. Of what use is half a lung or heart or womb? Such mutations would not survive birth, much less live to find sexually compatible mutations with the ability to reproduce. To ignore this obvious fact of the "present" in pursuit of the "past" is not rational, and it is certainly not scientific. It is long past time for the scientific world to view the "wisdom" of men from God's perspective:

> When I came to you, brothers, I did not come with eloquence or superior wisdom as I proclaimed to you the testimony about God. For I resolved to know nothing while I was with you except Jesus Christ and him crucified. I came to you in weakness and fear, and with much trembling. My message and my preaching were not with wise and persuasive words, but with a demonstration of the Spirit's power, so that your faith might not rest on men's wisdom, but on God's power...Do not deceive yourselves. If any one of you thinks he is wise **by the standards of this age**, he should become a "fool" so that he may become wise. For the wisdom of this world is foolishness in God's sight. As it is written: "He catches the wise in their craftiness"; and again, "The Lord knows that the thoughts of the wise are futile" (1 Corinthians 2:1-5; 3:18-20).

In recent years several authors have written popular books on human origins which were based more on fantasy and subjectivity than on fact and objectivity.[28]

28.   R. Martin, "Man is not an onion." *New Scientist*, 4 August 1977, page 283.

CHAPTER SIX

Uniquely Human

RICHARD LEAKEY IS ONE OF THE MOST RECOGNIZED NAMES IN THE
science of anthropology. Both of his parents, Louis and Mary Leakey, gave him a
literal birthright into a study of fossil remains. His book, *The Origin of
Humankind*, available in most local libraries, is only one of many excellent
resources on the subject. And even though he and many other anthropologists,
paleontologists and biologists believe that humans evolved from primate ancestors, most are exceptionally candid in presenting the difficulties involved in constructing such a theory. Mr. Leakey, in commenting on a difference of opinion
between Milford Wolpoff and Christopher Stringer, both recognized authorities, wrote:

> *These examples illustrate the problems anthropologists face. Not
> only are there differences of opinion over the significance of impor-
> tant anatomical features, but Neanderthals aside, the fossil record
> is much slimmer than most anthropologists would like (and most
> non-anthropologists believe). Until these impediments are overcome, a*

consensus on the larger question may remain out of reach (Richard
Leakey, *The Origin of Humankind*, Published by Basic Books, 1994, page 89).

Regardless of this comment, Mr. Leakey himself makes it very clear he
believes there is sufficient fossil evidence to show that man evolved from a
common ancestral tree that shows hominids on one path and the larger pri-
mates on another. The Leakey family and many others did not dream up
these human-like fossils. They exist! How long ago they existed may be
open to question, but there is nothing in Leakey's writings or any other
author that offers substantive evidence that these creatures are the ancestors of modern humans. On the contrary, **an objective view of the evidence** would lead one to believe that we are, albeit very late, a unique
creation by the living God. A species, like all others, that suddenly and
without naturalistic explanation just appeared.

We do not have to dig very far to find that fossil scientists have a ten-
dency to be extremely gifted in their ability to weave some pretty good stories from a scant or even nonexistent fossil record—even inventing
evidence. Piltdown Man fooled the fossil scientists for over forty years. He
was supposed to represent "an ancient form of man who lived as long as a
million years ago" (*World Book Encyclopedia*). The fraud was not discovered
until 1953. It turned out to be the skull of a modern ape. How was this
possible? **Because mental paradigms can blind us so that we only see
what we want to see!** Jesus encountered this in the religious community.
It is just as prevalent in the scientific community where "though seeing,
they do not see; though hearing, they do not hear or understand"
(Matthew 13:13).

Evidence, **actual reliable evidence**, shows that those things which
make modern humans unique, such as technological inventiveness, artistic
imaginations, and our sense of religion and morality are just a few thousand years old. Even using questionable dating technologies, the earliest
evidence of writing skills is only about six thousand years old. Evidence of
concentrated agricultural activity about ten thousand years, artistic expression a few thousand years earlier. Such facts are freely acknowledged by
Richard Leakey:

*Go back beyond this, however—beyond about 35,000 years ago—
and these beacons of the modern human mind gutter out* (Richard
Leakey, *The Origin of Humankind*, Published by Basic Books, 1994, page 80).

So what does the evidence show? **Modern humans are unique! They
have not been around very long!** The most devout evolutionists acknowledge these two facts. The real issue then, the focus of debate, the only thing
from which evolutionary theories about the human family are derived, is
whether or not anatomical similarities and rudimentary skills are satisfactory methods for adducing humanness in creatures that lived in the remote
past.

That we are similar to a gorilla cannot be denied. In fact, we are so close
in appearance we may feel like saying "howdy" every time we go to the zoo.
Most of a chimpanzee's DNA, about 99 percent, is the same as a human.
One cannot watch *National Geographic* or a similar type telecast without
being amazed at the ingenuity, the rudimentary intelligence, of such pri-
mates. However, **such behavior is not limited to animals anatomically
and genetically similar to humans!** Consider the fruit fly and its DNA
similarity to ours—or tropical ant colonies that protect certain beetles like
we do a herd of cattle. We milk our cattle. They milk their beetles.

Or consider the house the beaver builds. It's a better-engineered structure than many of those found among tribes of human beings. Several years
ago, a rancher, after several attempts to dam a creek, brought in a beaver.
The lake is still there. Beavers not only build good houses but also create
their own burglar deterrents and escape moats in the process.

Many stories about animal intelligence are also amusing, like the fox
that invariably found the tie chain and threw the trapper's trap. Or the dog
that, paddled with a house shoe for chasing cars, hid the shoe at a neighbor's house. He was not taught to do this. He figured it out on his own.
Others are not amusing. Like young elephants that, taken from their parents and turned loose without adult supervision in another park in South
Africa, became a violent gang of hoodlums. Attacking tourists. Killing rhi-
nos. This continued until a "big brother" program brought in some older,
adult elephants that very quickly established a viable social order.

Those at all familiar with ravens and crows know there are few things
they can't figure out in order to survive under extremely adverse conditions,

including the ability to coordinate work in groups that involve the art of deception and observation that approach human ingenuity. The number and variety of stories about such abilities in corvines, and in many other significantly different species, dismiss the concept that physical similarities and very rudimentary intelligence can ever be a basis for assigning modern humans to a long and evolving process.

That there were human-like creatures some time in the past is acknowledged. That they may have walked upright as we do is acknowledged. That, in some cases, they had a brain cavity close to ours is also acknowledged. That their DNA may be close to ours is acknowledged. But consider the number of species that may have inhabited the earth and these similarities would almost certainly be found in one or more of them:

> *There have been between 980 million and 1 billion species since the beginning of life on earth. There are over 4.5 million species currently living* (Dr. Homer W. Parker, Sr., Evolution Of Man Since The Earth Was Created, Page 5).

This means, if these estimates are correct, that about 99.5 percent of all species are now extinct. Even if grossly exaggerated the number is still staggering. Why, then, should it be thought illogical for some extinct creature to have been anatomically similar to modern humans? Or that some may have buried their dead? Dogs bury food. Cats bury their own waste. Why would a species have to be "human" just because they applied the same instincts to disposal of a dead body? And why should a species be called "human" simply because they may have had some rudimentary skills similar to ours? Regardless of some particular similarity or trait, as previously cited from Richard Leakey's book, those things that make modern humans a unique species cannot be assigned to such creatures. **Thinking to the contrary is based on wishful thinking and unproved assumptions!**

To illustrate the difficulty encountered in trying to reconstruct the trail of modern man, we need look no further than Cro-Magnon and Neanderthal. The long-standing assumption that Cro-Magnon and Neanderthal were related may have been wrong. Though somewhat anatomically similar, most scientists now believe they cannot be linked ancestrally, though evidence indicates they probably overlapped, even living in the same area at the same time. Yet there is no evidence of social or sexual interaction, a trait that exists in every human regardless of physical dissimilarities. Now, DNA tests seem to confirm they were not the same:

> *There are no known human fossils from western Europe that provide an evolutionary link between Neanderthal Man and the Cro-Magnon people...because the evidence now suggests that Neanderthal Man overlapped with Cro-Magnon Man in western Europe, the Neanderthals could not be direct ancestors of the first Cro-Magnon people* (Leslie Aiello, *Discovering The Origins Of Man*, Stonehenge Press Inc., Publisher: John Canova, Editor: Ezra Bowen, Trewin Copplestone Books, Ltd., page 76).

> *Genetic differences indicate the Neanderthals were a different species from the early humans who swept them aside in Europe and western Asia.... Their finding gives powerful backing to the theory that all humanity descended from an "African Eve" about 100,000 to 200,000 years ago* (The Associated Press, as reported by *The Kansas City Star*, July 11, 1997).

But not all scientists and researchers agree with this assessment. Erik Trinkaus, professor of Arts & Sciences, of Washington University in St. Louis, Missouri, believes the skeleton of a 24,500-year-old child was born to an early modern human and a Neanderthal.[29] And in *Buried Alive*, Jack Cuozzo, an orthodontist, challenges the theory that Neanderthals were less than modern humans. He believes that the teeth and jaw structure of Neanderthals, as depicted in models and drawings, has been altered to reflect more of an ape-like position. This, he says, has been done by the scientific community in spite of the fact that the actual skulls reflect orthodontic jaw and teeth patterns pretty much like Cro-Magnon.

Whether or not Neanderthal was a part of the human family may never be answered to everyone's satisfaction. They appear to have been heavily built with a brain cavity about the same as modern people. They lived primarily in Europe and parts of Asia, according to questionable dating techniques,

---

29. *Washington University Magazine*, Fall 1999, page 3.

about thirty thousand to over one hundred thousand years ago. They were hunters and gatherers, living in caves, with evidence they made crude tools from rocks. But there is little or no evidence they understood or practiced any kind of agricultural or religious activity.

On the other hand, the Cro-Magnon people made highly crafted and efficient tools and weapons from bone and flint. They produced art forms, both sculpted and painted. There is also evidence that they probably had some form of religious belief. The earliest generally assumed date for their appearance is about thirty-five to forty thousand years ago. Some have theorized that other types of human remains have been found and dated as much as one to two hundred thousand years ago. But the fossil and archaeological records to support this extrapolation are extremely meager and certainly inconclusive. Moreover, such conclusions, like previous Neanderthal theories, are highly suspect:

> You read statements to the effect that such and such a society or archeological site is 20,000 years old. We learned rather abruptly that these numbers, these ancient ages, are not known accurately (Science, "Radiocarbon Dating," by W. F. Libby, March 3, 1961, page 624).

The debate within the scientific community as to the relationship of Neanderthal and Cro-Magnon illustrates the difficulty in finding the truth about the past, including dating technologies that are inherently dependent on some level of **assumption** that inhibits accurate reconstruction of prehistorical time frames—which makes it difficult to dismiss as out of hand the contention by many creation scientists that all of these dates have been grossly exaggerated. But whatever and whenever it happened, there is, when all is said and done, that nagging, insurmountable problem—the lack of sufficient fossil evidence to support traditional theories that modern humans evolved from lower life forms:

> The origin of humanity has been claimed as being in Asia, Africa and even the whole world at the same time. The human record has been investigated as intensively as any, but there are still enormous holes in it.... Whatever the merits of each doctrine there are so many gaps in the human fossil record that there is just not enough information to tell

whether humans evolved suddenly or slowly (Steve Jones, *The Language of Genes*, Anchor Books, Bantam Doubleday Dell Publishing Group, Inc., 1540 Broadway, New York, NY 10036, pages 102, 106).

The fact that there is **"not enough information to tell"** is, in and of itself, strong and compelling evidence that the **assumed** links between modern humans and lesser creatures is based on wishful thinking. But many scientists, rather than admit that fossil and archaeological evidence show that humans suddenly and recently appeared, evade the obvious conclusion. They can't seem to break through their paradigm of thought that excludes the concept of **creative differences** between modern humans and other species. Such evidence becomes even more believable when one considers our inherent spiritual nature, the need for a god, the need for immortality. It may not be measurable like a gallon of water, but who has not felt this need? It is a need overtly expressed in worship. **No such attribute exists in any other species!**

So why have our school systems and educational media bought into current evolutionary theories? **Political correctness!** Which is simply a method for suppressing the truth to achieve a political or social objective. Until recently, it was used in educational textbooks to grossly distort and suppress the truth about the history and contribution of Black, Hispanic and Asian people to the human family—even depicting Native Americans as savages to justify their slaughter, appropriation of their lands, and elimination of their cultures. In the same "politically correct" vein and with unmitigated fervor, educational media openly declare that evolutionary naturalism is a fact, including the evolution of humans. This is especially distressing when the **open secret within the scientific community itself is that the doctrine is lacking in credible fossil evidence:**

> *When writing in scientific journals, leading biologists candidly discuss many scientific difficulties facing contemporary versions of Darwin's theory. Yet when these same scientists take on the public defense of Darwinism—in educational policy statements and textbooks—that* **candor disappears behind a rhetorical curtain** (Stephen C. Meyer, Director of Discovery Institute's Center for the Renewal of Science and Culture, in a special article for the *Kansas City Star*, 10-16-00, emphasis added).

There's a feeling in biology that scientists should keep their dirty laundry hidden...there's a strong school of thought in biology that one should never question Darwin in public (Danny Hillis, biologist, as quoted in the same article).

Stephen Gould, an eminent Harvard professor and devout evolutionist, also quoted in the *Star* article, openly acknowledges that embryological drawings in textbooks are "fraudulent." And that "we have the right to be both astonished and ashamed by...the persistence of these drawings in a large number, if not the majority, of modern textbooks." Whether influenced by religion, politics, science or perceived social need, this penchant for teaching outright untruths and shading historical facts has always been a problem for educational systems throughout the world. If this is not an attempt to perpetuate ignorance of a "position" that cannot stand public scrutiny, what would you call it?

But there is reason to hope for something better. Even now, scientists and Native Americans are at odds over a "politically correct" hot potato— evidence that some original settlers of North and South America do not fit the long-held theory that they all came over a land bridge between Asia and North America. The first to advance the idea that this theory was wrong was a man named Tom Dillehay, an archaeologist at the University of Kentucky. For years he was dismissed and even shunned by the scientific community for his findings at a site called Monte Verde, which, he said, predated all others by about one thousand years. But "that changed two years ago, when archaeology's pooh-bahs finally accepted that Monte Verde was indeed 12,500 years old. The floodgates opened...we are rewriting the textbooks on the First Americans" (*Newsweek*, April 26, 1999, pages 54-58). Other sites are revealing even earlier and more startling results—the probability that original Americans did not come by one route or from one group of people. Some may have even been Europeans.

Whatever the results, it emphasizes the dilemma often faced by both the scientific and religious communities—**admission of error!** In this case, it only involves the unrelated issue of the peopling of America. But in the case of Darwinism there is a lot more at stake—the whole concept of evolution! Yet, as in the case just discussed, the floodgates are beginning to crack. Darwinism, even updated versions, may still be politically correct, but more and more scientists, as well as many educators, are beginning to acknowledge the inevitable conclusion that it simply **does not fit the evidence!** Neither for evolution in general nor humans in particular:

> *I believe that one day the Darwinian myth will be ranked the greatest deceit in the history of science. When this happens many people will pose the question: how did this ever happen?* (Saltationist Soren Lovtrup, Professor of Embryology, University of UMFA, Sweden; *Darwinism, The Refutation of a Myth* [New York: Chapman Hall, 1987], page 422).

> *We have had enough of the Darwinian fallacy. It's about time we cry "the emperor has no clothes"* (Ken Hsu, Geological Institute of Zurich, Former President of the International Association of Sedimentologists; "Darwin's Three Mistakes," *Geology*, volume 14 [1986], page 534).

Evolutionary naturalism is not just about the idea that we are related to a look-alike primate. It also means that the frog and poison ivy are our cousins. That, dear friends, is what we are asked to believe. Personally, I prefer God! And the evidence!

Do nothing out of selfish ambition or vain conceit, but in humility consider others better than yourselves.

Philippians 2:3

CHAPTER SEVEN

Evolution and Racism

THERE IS A VERY REAL SOCIAL PROBLEM INHERENT IN TRADITIONAL evolutionary theories—racism! Such theories have proved to be fertile soil for this insidious evil. Roger Lewin identified this human depravity in his book, *Bones of Contention*:

> *The brain of the Negro is that of the imperfect brain of a seven-month infant in the womb of a white...Racism, as we would characterize it today, was explicit in the writings of virtually all the major anthropologists of the first decades of this century, simply because it was the generally accepted world view* (Roger Lewin, *Bones of Contention*, pages 306-7).

What ignorance! And it was **perpetuated by the scientific community** simply because it was the **"generally accepted"** theory! The obvious fact that many of the brightest and ablest among us are not Caucasian was simply ignored by those who are not supposed to be swayed by popular thinking—scientists! This is a red flag of monumental proportions. Greed and lust for power and superiority have always brought out those who seek justification for mistreatment and abuse of those who by race, features, physical or mental disability, or economic or educational circumstance, have been disenfranchised:

> *The founder of Social Darwinism, the idea that poverty and wealth are inevitable as they represent the biological rules which govern society, was the philosopher Herbert Spencer...who used The Origin Of Species as a rationale for the excesses of nineteenth-century capitalism. The steel magnate Andrew Carnegie was impressed by the idea that evolution excuses injustice. He invited Herbert Spencer to Pittsburgh. The philosopher's response to seeing his theories worked out in steel and concrete was that "six months residence here would justify suicide"* (Steve Jones, The Language of Genes, Anchor Books, Bantam Doubleday Dell Publishing Group, Inc., 1540 Broadway, New York, NY 10036, page 17).

It is one thing to advance philosophies. They're just words. But, as Spencer found out, his words were used for purposes never intended—justification for actions that produce caste systems of the most despicable kind. He was appalled at the misery of those at the bottom of the pile—especially painful because he was directly responsible for giving sanction, although not intended, to such inhumane conditions.

But everyone is not conscience stricken. Charles Darwin's cousin, Francis Galton, "was all in favor of interfering with human evolution. He supported the idea of breeding them from the best and sterilizing those whose inheritance did not meet with his approval"[30]—a philosophy that many people think originated with Adolph Hitler.

A man named Ernst Haeckel used Galton's ideas and Darwin's book, *The Origin of Species*, as the basis for establishing the Monist League in Germany prior to the First World War. Thousands of Germans became members, dedicating themselves to advancement of doctrines declaring the superiority of a select group of white Europeans. Such irrationality prepared the soil for Adolph Hitler, the mad man who started World War 2.

---

30. Steve Jones, *The Language of Genes*, Anchor Books, Bantam Doubleday Dell Publishing Group, Inc., 1540 Broadway, New York, NY 10036, pages 15-17.

He, like others before him, latched on to the idea of a "super race" based on Darwinian theories. To make this happen, he invoked the holocaust, the systematic extermination of undesirables. Jews and the disabled, including non-Jewish German citizens, were specifically targeted.

It's true that religion has also been used to justify the elimination of those who are different. But whether derived from evolutionary theories or imbedded in religious doctrines, the result is the same. The difference, however, is that evolutionary naturalism is taught as an unassailable truth by public schools and publicly supported media outlets.

How different racial characteristics came to be is answered neither by the Bible nor by science. There is much speculation but no proof. The only thing we know for sure is that **mental capacity is racially neutral.** Any postulating to the contrary is without either scientific or Biblical foundation. Whether born in a remote jungle or in the lap of luxury, two babies, if healthy and taken at birth and placed in the same environment, will probably mature and learn at about the same rate. If there is a difference, the more advanced is as likely as not to have come from the jungle. The odds of such balanced mentality occurring in different evolutionary trees are too enormous to comprehend. On the other hand, the odds are just as enormous, **based on credible, physical evidence,** of both babies being related, just as the Bible says, to a common ancestor:

> From one man he made every nation of men, that they should inhabit the whole earth; and he determined the times set for them and the exact places where they should live (Acts 17:26).

The idea of a super race, of one race being superior to another because of the color of their skin, is sheer nonsense. **It is pure ignorance!** The skin of all people consists of the same ingredients. Those with yellowish skin have more "carotene" pigment than do so-called white people. Those with darker skins have more of the "melanin" pigment. But everyone's skin, regardless of his or her race, from the whitest to the darkest, is affected. As a result, we are all alike. We are all "colored!" Except for a rare physical condition called albinism, there is no such thing as a "white" person. The only difference is the shade of color based on variable quantities of each pigment. One is not a blessing from God any more than another.

Racial ignorance has even prompted some to believe that Adam and Eve were white. That isn't even a good assumption. Common sense tells us it was probably just the opposite. The weather was so warm they were able to live without benefit of clothing—"naked." Those with light-colored skin are far less biologically suited for this condition than those with darker skin pigmentation.

Also overlooked in this volatile issue by racists, who often misquote the Bible to justify their selfish and arrogant ambitions, is the genetic structure that allows interracial breeding between people of all color and features—**a fact that proves beyond doubt that God Himself considers us one and the same!** If not, He would have made it genetically impossible for the offspring of an interracial couple to reproduce. In fact, there is a greater DNA variation within a race than between the races (*Reader's Digest*, November 2000, page 83).

But there is something else that far transcends the racial issue—gene identification and manipulation. Never before have we had to face an issue of such moral importance. With the ability to know about genetically inheritable traits, including the potential for serious health problems, there will be an unavoidable desire to prevent copulation between two unsuitable sexual partners or to destroy any fetal result. There will also be an overwhelming temptation to alter the genetic makeup to eliminate certain characteristics or produce more desirable ones. This is not science fiction. The technology now exists and is expanding daily. Couple this with the moral depravity to which men can sink and the danger is quite evident. History is filled with the names of those who supported the idea of sterilizing or killing those not meeting some particular criteria.

No one should deny that there are countless benefits to gene manipulation, especially the ability to remove from the genetic chain those inheritable traits that cause mental and physical disabilities. But an evolutionary theory that gives us no higher reason than ourselves to avoid abuse of modern medicines and technologies is a very dangerous doctrine. It not only rationalizes whatever the rich and powerful choose to do, but gives them a heretofore unknown technology to make it happen. It may also result in new species of animals and plants that do far more harm than good.

The danger is real. Modern technology has already made it possible to murder the unborn at an assembly line pace. The only justification is that they are "not wanted." They are not "convenient." They interfere with "my rights." They do not have to possess defective genes. They only have to meet someone's definition of an "undesirable." Like a piece of scrap, they are removed from the womb and tossed out with the garbage. Anyone who doubts that **God considers abortion to be an act of taking someone's life** is in a state of denial:

> For he did not **kill** me in the womb, with my mother as my **grave** (Jeremiah 20:17).

The word, "kill," is from a "primitive root: to die (literally or figuratively); **causatively**, to kill."[31] It is the same Hebrew word used to record Pharaoh's command to kill all male children born to Hebrew mothers (Exodus 1:16), and of Saul's plan to **murder** David (1 Samuel 19:1). It was even used to describe the accidental killing of a grown man (Deuteronomy 19:5). It is a word that always means **to take the life of a living person**, child and adult alike.

If this is not enough to convince you that the purpose of abortion is to commit murder, I suggest you read the article written by George F. Will, *Newsweek*, October 2, 2000. He is commenting on the Born-Alive Infants Protection Act, designed to protect the right to life of "infants who survive abortions." Those opposing this protective act would give the mother the right to kill the child **as much as a month after birth!** Cover it up anyway you like, the bottom line is that pro-choice measures are essentially designed "as a matter of protecting consumer rights—a woman purchasing an abortion is entitled to a dead baby." Whether in or out of the womb!

Put yourself in an abortion clinic. Watch and listen as the fetus is removed. "She's still breathing," says the doctor. "What shall I do," says the nurse. "Throw it in the trash," says the doctor. "Wait," says the nurse. "Let's ask Him." Then you notice someone standing in the shadows. "Who is that," the doctor asks. "Jesus," is her reply. You wait, watching as He comes closer. He bends down, looks at the small struggling child, and says to the nurse, "Go ahead, kill her." You don't believe that anymore than I do. So let

---

31. (Biblesoft's New Exhaustive Strong's Numbers and Concordance with Expanded Greek-Hebrew Dictionary. Copyright (c) 1994, Biblesoft and International Bible Translators, Inc.).

me remind those who are party to these horrible acts of genocide, God is watching **AND TAKING NOTES!** You may not see Him but **HE KNOWS** every little detail of what goes on in the world:

> *Where can I go from your Spirit?* ***Where can I flee from your presence?*** *If I go up to the heavens, you are there; if I make my bed in the depths, you are there...even the darkness will not be dark to you...For you* ***created*** *my inmost being;* ***you knit me together in my mother's womb...*** *When I was woven together in the depths of the earth* ***your eyes saw my unformed body*** (Psalm 139:7-16).

The word "created" comes from "a primitive root; to erect, i.e. create ...by implication to own."[32] Abortion is an act of destruction against what God, as the Creator of natural law, "knit together." The context clearly shows that from the "unformed body," in its most elemental, constituent parts, to an adult person, God **sees**, through His omniscient power, the formation and development of life. By any reasonable criteria, **conception brings and joins together all necessary genetic elements of life!** Attachment of the fertilized egg to the uterine wall then turns the mother into a "life-support system." Abortion, which "disconnects" that life, is no different and no less wrong than "pulling the plug" on a comatose person who has every chance of full recovery. An act every court in America would consider premeditated murder.

How, then, can pregnant women, and support groups who approve and even encourage their abortive actions, justify their actions? Who gave them the right to consider that which God "created" and "owns" a disposable "fetus," a thing of "choice"? No president, no governor, no legislature, no court "under God" has the authority to "approve" of this heinous defiance of His laws. Temporal gratification will mean nothing on the Day of Judgment (Mark 8:37):

> For we must all appear before the judgment seat of Christ, that each one may receive what is due him for the things done while in the body, whether good or bad... "It is mine to avenge; **I will repay**" ...It is a

---

32. *Biblesoft's New Exhaustive Strong's Numbers and Concordance with Expanded Greek-Hebrew Dictionary.* Copyright (c) 1994, Biblesoft and International Bible Translators, Inc.

dreadful thing to fall into the hands of the living God (2 Corinthians
5:10; Hebrews 10:30-31).

But wholesale abortion is just the beginning of modern medical atroc-
ities. If history teaches us anything at all about human responses, anyone
with less than a desirable genetic chain should be very concerned, especially
since "desirable" is a floating definition, depending on who's in a position to
enforce compliance. We know from past experience that a few scientists
have always been willing to apply their knowledge to advance their own
social agenda, or, for enough money, the social, political or profit motives of
someone else. The rewards from genetic manipulation can be substantial
and alluring:

> *Because wealth and social position depend so much on descent the rich*
> *were the first geneticists…. There is a fresh danger that genetics will*
> *be used as an excuse to discriminate against the handicapped in order*
> *to save money…. The explosion in knowledge means that society will*
> *soon, like it or not, be faced with ethical problems of the kind compre-*
> *hensively ignored by the founders of eugenics* (Steve Jones, The Language
> of Genes, Anchor Books, Bantam Doubleday Dell Publishing Group, Inc.,
> 1540 Broadway, New York, NY 10036, pages 29, 26, 225).

In St. Louis, Missouri, on the campus of Washington University, sits a
little-noticed building housing the greatest scientific endeavor in the history of the world—the Human Genome Project. Its primary objective is to
mark the exact order of the six billion pieces that make up human DNA.
The ultimate scientific goal is to understand why we are what we are, and
how we can control and change ourselves. They are not the only one pursuing this goal. The winners may even have the legal right to patent their
discoveries with unimaginable abilities to control genetic manipulation.
The troubling trend of assessing "genetic risk" will only get worse as
employers and insurance companies enhance their ability to look at the
entire genetic structure of every applicant.

With such immoral realities, we should be obsessed with keeping spiritual guidelines in public education. **This does not mean** public school systems should advocate any one religious doctrine over another. But it doesn't

take a genius to know that such things as "doing to others as you would have them do to you" can be taught without crossing the line. We should also demand that our school systems teach the whole truth about creation versus evolution so that our children's future will not be based on incomplete information and "politically correct" opinions that endure simply because they are "generally accepted." Even some evolutionists agree this is a logical and sensible approach to a better understanding of the issues:

> No teacher should be dismayed at efforts to present creation as an alternative to evolution in biology courses; indeed, at this moment creation is the only alternative to evolution. Not only is this worth mentioning, but a comparison of the two alternatives can be an excellent exercise in logic and reason. Our primary goal as educators should be to teach students to think, and such a comparison, particularly because it concerns an issue in which many have special interests or are even emotionally involved, may accomplish that purpose better than others (R. D. Alexander, Evolution versus Creationism: The Public Education Controversy, editor J. P. Zetterberg [Phoenix: Oryx Press, 1983], page 91).

Statements like the following not only meet the test of scientific "logic and reason" but inherently encourage students to seek spiritual answers for moral guidance outside the classroom in a religion of their own choice:

+ **Science cannot explain how nature began.**
+ **Science cannot explain how new species appeared.**
+ **Dating technologies are inherently flawed.**
+ **Modern humans are unique and recent.**
+ **Evolution justifies "survival of the fittest" ideologies.**
+ **Genetic manipulation must be carefully contained.**

It is no lack of coincidence that removal of the concept of a Supreme Being from our classrooms has been followed by an unrivaled decline in morality and increase in violent behavior. Evolutionary theories have been used to reduce human beings to the level of pure physical form without any spiritual consequences. Why, then, should we not "eat, drink and be merry" and "do to others before they do to us"? It is pure folly to think that government or scientific agendas can control a free society without spiritual affections. It is the very heart of democracy:

> *Reason and experience forbid us to expect that national morality can prevail in exclusion of religious principle* (George Washington, First President of the United States).

> *We hold these truths to be self-evident, that all men are created equal, that they are endowed by their Creator with certain inalienable Rights, that among them are Life, Liberty and the pursuit of Happiness* (Declaration of Independence).

In spite of these founding principles, we have consciously and deliberately removed God from our institutions. The result is crystal clear. We have lost our moral compass. This is not subjective philosophy. It's a reality we are experiencing every day, even in our schools where the joy of youth and serenity of a dedicated learning environment have been replaced with fear and armed guards:

> *This may be one of the first generations in history not to pass on its moral teachings to its young people. Hollywood is not helping. Schools are not dealing with it. Even parents have lost their nerve.*[33]

History resounds with the fact that all nations, which lost their sense of morality, have fallen. As trite as it may sound to some, as old-fashioned as the words may be, such destruction has always been and still is God's judgment against sin. He has judged us and we have come up short:

> *If you ever forget the LORD your God and follow other gods and worship and bow down to them, I testify against you today that you will surely be destroyed. Like the nations the LORD destroyed before you, so you will be destroyed for not obeying the LORD your*

---

33. A quotation of Christina Hoff Sommers, associate professor of philosophy at Clark University, Worchester, Massachusetts, by Cheryl Downey, *Orange Coast* (December '96), 245-D Fischer Avenue, Costa Mesa, California 92626.

God... [for] righteousness exalts a nation, but sin is a disgrace to any people (Deuteronomy 8:19-20; Proverbs 14:34).

In spite of our wealth, in spite of our knowledge, perhaps because of it, we are rapidly becoming a sinful, unhappy people. It is a statistical fact too serious to disregard. In the past few decades, we have sought happiness from philosophers, astrologers, scientists, off-beat religionists, sexual deviates, guns, games, entertainers, physical appearances, and other obsessions too numerous to mention. Yet any honest person must surely conclude that neither physical pleasure nor science nor religions of human origin has given us the right answers.

It is time to discard the worthless and accept the incomparable gift of eternal life expressed in the death and resurrection of God's Son, Jesus Christ! Only then, **if we adhere to His teachings**, can we come to know that every person, of every country, of every race, born and unborn, is not our evolutionary lesser but an **equal relative** of a common ancestor, "created in the image of God" (Genesis 1:26-27):

> *From one man he made every nation of men"* (Acts 17:26) ... *So in everything, do to others what you would have them do to you* (Matthew 7:12) ... *Therefore, as we have opportunity, let us do good to all people, especially to those who belong to the family of believers"* (Galatians 6:10).

How could anyone read such Scriptures and feel they were superior, much less part of a "super race"? Such an uncharitable social attitude can survive only if one cherishes evolution over equal creation by a Supreme Being we call GOD and His manifestation in the person of Jesus Christ.

Wisdom is supreme; therefore get wisdom.

Though it cost all you have, get understanding.

Esteem her, and she will exalt you; embrace her, and she will honor you.

She will set a garland of grace on your head and present you with a crown of splendor.

Proverbs 4:7-9

Epilog

ALL THEORIES REGARDING THE AGE OF THE EARTH AND ITS CREATURES, including humans, are based, at the most fundamental level, on **unprovable assumptions**! And theories that discount a creative God are inherently unscientific. For no scientific theory will ever be able to demonstrate how nature **began** without the influence of a **supernatural power**! Yet, in spite of these facts, many scientists, over the last hundred years, have declared that God was dead, evolution was a fact, science would supply the answers to all questions, and all but the "ignorant" would discard religion as mere superstition.

So what happened? Most educated people of the world still believe in God. Presidents still humble themselves before Him. And an increasing number of scientists are acknowledging there must be something "out there!" Even Russia and China, those fading bastions of godless Communism, have now embarked on government-sponsored efforts to educate their people in the English language, **using the Christian Bible as a textbook!**

Why has this happened? We have learned more about science than the "God is dead" prognosticators ever envisioned. So why has the idea of God not faded away? Because humans are more than animated piles of flesh, blood and bones. **We are also a spiritual creation!** Try as we might, we are unable to detach ourselves from our Creator. There is a spiritual connection that science will never be able to measure or analyze or destroy.

Yet, in spite of this spiritual connection, this inability to break free, we still spurn His instructions for Godly living. We invent compromises that give us the illusion of maintaining a relationship with Him but in reality reject His holy commandments. As it was in the time of Jesus, so it is today. We're just better at it, more educated, more sophisticated, in deviant philosophies. Including evolutionary doctrines which, by their very nature, have become an insidious and pervasive part of these philosophies. The cavalier attitude about abortion is a ghastly example of this dehumanizing effect on our conscience.

It doesn't work! Fence straddling, one foot in the world and the other in the church, is **unacceptable** (Matthew 23:27-28). It is time to awaken to the danger of these spiritually destructive viruses of the mind. It is time to review our conduct and stir up our conscience. To seek out truth and commit our lives, **mind, soul and body**, to that truth (Matthew 22:37-40). It is that "truth," the truth that will "set you free" (John 8:32), that I have endeavored to reveal in this book.

Now it is up to you. First, do what the Bereans did. They "examined the Scriptures" to determine for themselves whether or not the things the messenger taught were true (Acts 17:11). Then build on that knowledge. Use public and religious libraries and other resources that will enhance your understanding of historical and natural evidences. When you are finished, I think you will find that the following statements reflect some fundamental beliefs you can stick on your refrigerator and absorb into your life:

+ **Jesus Christ is the Son of God.**
+ **Salvation is found only in Jesus Christ.**
+ **The Bible is God's "spiritual message" to humanity.**
+ **The Bible reveals a supernatural "Creator."**
+ **Nature reveals a supernatural "Creator."**
+ **No one knows "when" creation took place.**
+ **All people are "equal" in the sight of God.**

But these are only facts. And facts, unless translated into action, give little comfort to the addict who needs help. As does the new divorcee who feels betrayed and alone, the brokenhearted mother whose child has just been killed by a drunk driver, and the driver who wishes he were dead instead. Or the fifty-year-old man who just lost his job. Or the child who is starving to death. Or those who have been attacked physically or verbally because of their religion, race, disability or ethnicity. Such people are hurting! They need compassion and understanding. This is where Christians come in. **They are the ambassadors of Christ!** By reaching out to those in need, as He did, they express a greater testimony about the reality of Christ than all the historical and archaeological evidence in the world. Through Christians, **through their lifestyles,** God becomes personal and involved.

And so, above all things, I pray that all Christians will become more concerned with being faithful ambassadors in deed than with a recitation of facts—that through their lifestyles they will lead others to Christ. That they may also experience the enriching power of Him who said, "Come to me, all you who are weary and burdened, and I will give you rest. Take my yoke upon you and learn from me, for I am gentle and humble in heart, and you will find rest for your souls. For my yoke is easy and my burden is light" (Matthew 11:28-30). Jesus lived for us! Jesus died for us! He is able to give us peace that passes understanding and to comfort us when we are in need:

> *Do not be anxious about anything, but in everything, by prayer and petition, with thanksgiving, present your requests to God. And the peace of God, which transcends all understanding, will guard your hearts and your minds in Christ Jesus* (Philippians 4:6-7).

> *Therefore, since we have a great high priest who has gone through the heavens, Jesus the Son of God, let us hold firmly to the faith we profess. For we do not have a high priest who is unable to sympathize with our weaknesses, but we have one who has been tempted in every way, just as we are—yet was without sin. Let us then approach the throne of grace with confidence, so that we may receive mercy and find grace to help us in our time of need* (Hebrews 4:14-16).

That we all need His "peace…mercy and grace" in this life is abundantly clear. But far transcending any calamity of life is that moment when we die—when death takes on a meaning that eludes all but those for whom it is imminent. For when the door of death opens to the unseeing blackness of eternity, what will we be thinking? That Jesus is there to walk with us through the "valley of the shadow of death?" Or that we must enter the realm of the dead alone, not knowing if it is the end of our existence or the beginning of eternal torment? Our predicament is the same as that of Robert Ingersoll, an eloquent nineteenth-century agnostic, who heard these haunting words from a gospel preacher:

> *Robert, if you are right and I am wrong, neither of us will ever know about it. But if I am right, and you are wrong, we will both know it throughout eternity.*

If you are not a Christian, may God bless you with an appropriate and unreserved response to the invitation of Jesus Christ, Son of the Living God! Make your decision in a prayerful, thoughtful and wise sense of who you now are—**and who you can become!** Remember, today is the first day of the rest of your life:

> *Forgetting what is behind and straining toward what is ahead, I press on toward the goal to win the prize for which God has called me heavenward in Christ Jesus* (Philippians 3:13-14).

If you are a Christian, comfortable with a particular belief about creation, it does not mean those you love have the same feelings. I know, from personal knowledge of those who have broken spiritual ties and from comments on this book by faithful, conservative members of the Lord's church, that this is undoubtedly the situation for millions of people. I'm sure you can personally name many who are now a part of this dreary statistic. Especially heartbreaking is the loss of our own children. This is why I have tried so hard, in a kind but honest and forthright manner, to show in this book that having different "opinions" about creation is not a reason to reject the authenticity of the Bible. I pray you will be like one father who said, "Thank you for letting me be one of the first to read your book. I want to buy a copy for each of my three sons when you have it published."

For those who have not yet become irreparably brainwashed by deception, please give them an opportunity, through an unbiased study of reliable and available evidence, to know that the Bible is God's spiritual message to the world; proclaiming that salvation is found only in Christ! And that evolutionist theories which dismiss the creative involvement of God are nothing more than human postulations—words without proof! Dangerous words that ultimately, overtly or covertly, diminish the crowning act of divine creation—man and woman—made in the image of God!

With that thought, I close this book with a comment made by Daniel Webster, one of America's greatest statesmen—a comment that defines holy and immortal objectives which are in stark contrast with the superficial and temporal wisdom of men:

*If we write on marble, it will perish; if on brass, time will efface it. If we rear temples, they will crumble into dust. But if we work on immortal minds, and imbue them with the just fear of God and love for their fellow man, we will write upon those tablets **something that will brighten all eternity!***

Respectfully presented for edification and strengthening in Christian faith, hope and love (1 Corinthians 13:13).

Calvin F. Fields
(913) 773-8216
www.thingsyouneverheard.com
31935 247th St.
Easton, KS 66020

A final thought: "My people are destroyed from lack of knowledge" (Hosea 4:6). If you bought or encouraged the purchase of this book for at least two additional people, and each succeeding level did the same thing, we could, within a very short period of time, sufficiently inform enough people to bring about a reduction in the number of abortions and changes in educators' views of evolution. Both are worthy objectives! As is the number of people whose morality in other ways may be enhanced, especially if they accept Jesus as their Savior!

Things You Never Heard
Order Form

Postal orders: Calvin Fields
31935 - 247th. Street
Easton, KS 66020

Telephone orders: (913) 773-8216

Please send *Things You Never Heard* to:

Name: _____

Address: _____

City: _____ State: _____

Zip: _____

Telephone: (_____) _____

Book Price: $11.00

Shipping: $3.00 for the first book and $1.00 for each additional book to
cover shipping and handling within US, Canada, and Mexico.
International orders add $6.00 for the first book and $2.00 for
each additional book

Or order from:
ACW Press
5501 N. 7th. Ave. #502
Phoenix, AZ 85013

(800) 931-BOOK

or contact your local bookstore